WHAT ARE THEY SAYING ABOUT
WISDOM LITERATURE?

What Are They Saying About Wisdom Literature?

Dianne Bergant, C.S.A.

PAULIST PRESS
New York/Ramsey

Acknowledgements

The Publisher gratefully acknowledges the use of excerpts from the following works:

God at Work in Israel by Gerhard von Rad. English translation reprinted by permission of Abingdon Press, Nashville, Tennessee. Originally published in German by Neukirchener Verlag, West Germany.
Israelite Wisdom, edited by John G. Gammie, Walter A. Brueggemann, W. Lee Humphreys and James M. Ward. Reprinted by permission of Scholars Press on behalf of Union Theological Seminary, New York.
The Intellectual Tradition in the Old Testament by R.N. Whybray (1974). Reprinted by permission of Walter de Gruyter & Company, Berlin.

Library of Congress
Catalog Card Number: 83-82027

ISBN: 0-8091-2605-2

Published by Paulist Press
545 Island Road, Ramsey, N.J. 07446

Printed and bound in the
United States of America

Contents

Preface

A study of the wisdom literature of biblical Israel can take several different directions. One can investigate salient ideas and trace their appearance and development throughout various biblical books. Or one can concentrate on a single work and study every theme found therein. Scholars have chosen both approaches and have published their findings accordingly. The present volume is an overview of significant authors who subscribe to either approach. Chapters 1, 2, and 7 will address three questions that are general in nature, while the remaining chapters will deal with one or, in the case of Chapter 6, two books of the Scriptures. Because the approach here is twofold, books which are representative of both categories will be examined.

Wisdom in Israel by Gerhard von Rad is a work of such importance that it is impossible to overlook it. This does not mean that more recent scholarship has not challenged some of its stands. One would consider it too fundamental to the study of wisdom to neglect giving it considerable attention. Although R.N. Whybray's treatment of wisdom material is not as extensive as von Rad's, his understanding of wisdom and its setting in Israel is important enough to include *The Intellectual Tradition in the Old Testament* in the present discussion.

Both *Studies in Ancient Israelite Wisdom* edited by James L. Crenshaw and *Israelite Wisdom* edited by John G. Gammie, Walter A. Brueggemann, W. Lee Humphreys, and James M. Ward contain numerous examples of scholarship both current and enduring. An examination of different articles from these collections will offer the reader a glimpse of the vast spectrum of scholarly concerns, methodological approaches, and resulting conclusions. The reader will then begin to appreciate how different they are.

1

1
Definition

A careful study of those books and texts that have come to be known as the wisdom material of the Hebrew Scriptures will reveal that the definition of this phenomenon which developed within ancient Israel is as diversified and elusive as the phenomenon itself. It has been variously referred to as: the meaning *in* life, the meaning *of* life, ancient humanism, the way to success, the discovery of the order of creation and conformity to them, etc. While there may be considerable correspondence in these various definitions, each focuses on the phenomenon from a slightly different standpoint and, thereby, affords a distinctive perspective. A closer examination of several of these definitions will reveal the differences within scholarly thought, but at the same time the multifaceted character of the wisdom perspective itself.

An Empirical Knowledge of Order

In his monumental work, *Old Testament Theology,* Gerhard von Rad installed "salvation history" as chief among the theological concepts of ancient Israel. Everything else assumed importance in relation to this preeminent theme. From the outset, wisdom posed a challenge to this arrangement. Its concerns were not historical; it did not highlight the saving acts of God in the lives of women and men. Where did wisdom fit within such a recital? Where should its

3

examination be placed within a treatise on such a history? Unable to consider it along with other covenantal concerns, von Rad placed it at the end of his treatment of the narrative sections of the biblical texts and entitled it "Israel's Response." This in itself has been criticized, for if the material provides no evidence of an interest in covenant, how can it be regarded as a response to it? Yet, while von Rad's placement and the title have been seriously questioned, the definition he gives for wisdom has been accepted by many. Von Rad views wisdom as "practical knowledge of the laws of life and of the world, based on experience."[1] This definition serves as framework for his study *Wisdom in Israel.*

One of the prominent themes of this work is "order," which can be discerned within creation as well as within the social mores of society. It was believed that success in life depended upon one's willingness and ability to discover this order and to live in harmony with it. The wise person was the one who succeeded at this in spite of the limitations with which one was faced. These limits will be discussed later. Here attention will be given to what was considered correct social behavior as well as to the order within creation.

According to von Rad, Israel "did not differentiate between a 'life wisdom' that pertained to the social orders and a 'natural wisdom,' because she was unable to objectify these spheres in the form of such abstractions."[2] This would explain why so much of the instruction exhorting people to proper conduct resorted to the animal world for examples of virtue, and why the regularity observable within the rhythms of nature was employed to reinforce confidence in the predicted consequences of certain actions. The sages of ancient Egypt taught that there was a basic "world order" Ma'at which regulated the cosmic world, the social world, as well as the world of the gods. Everything must accommodate itself to this "world order." While significantly adapting this concept, Israel's notion of "justice" or "righteousness" was influenced by it.

Goodness and evil were not merely qualities but were active forces that could be experienced.[3] When one chose good or evil it was released into the world and, because of some inherent determinism, effected good or evil respectively. Due to the unity of all reality, the good or evil consequences could be felt in the realm of social life or in that of nature. Understandably, the way to assure happiness and success in life was to leash the powers of evil and to set free those of good. Experience was the best teacher for distinguishing one from the other. Social mores, instructions and laws were the collected wisdom of the society, gleaned from the experience of the past. Adherence to them promised mastery of life and the rewards that this would bring, while disregard for them resulted in failure and unhappiness. It is against this backdrop that any theory of retribution should be understood. The good will be rewarded and the evil will be punished because of the inevitability of cause-and-effect.

The wisdom that has been described so far is the product of *NB* human reflection on human experience. It is conformity to the underlying "world order" and results in appropriate social and personal order in life. But what of the "world order" itself? Whence does it come? Who or what is responsible for its stability and endurance? As with the human wisdom, this phenomenon too has been variously defined by scholars. Nor do the biblical texts provide a uniform glimpse of it. Is it a superhuman creature? A divine attribute? A personification of God? A lesser deity? Von Rad has a most interesting explanation of this reality. He rejects the identification of wisdom either as a divine attribute or as a personification of God. He believes that this wisdom is within the world but beyond human grasp. "It is also something separate from the works of creation. This 'wisdom,' this 'understanding,' must, therefore, signify something like the 'meaning' implanted by God in creation, the divine mystery of creation."[4] This mystery always calls out to, always beckons to women and men, cajoling, enticing, challenging them to search out the secrets of creation and of life. And yet, as the wisdom poem in Job so accurately states, only "God understands the way to it," only God "knows its place" (28:23).

Although these two concepts of wisdom—the experiential and the mysterious—are distinct from one another, they are also intimately associated with each other. The first originates within human life and results from human reflection and conformity to perceived order. The second has its origin in God the Creator and consists of the primordial mystery of creation. Women and men in perpetual search of the latter will have to reconcile themselves with acquisition of the former. The coveted exceptional wisdom may have been hidden within creation far from human attainment, but order and regularity were not. They could be observed and, subsequently, predicted and could provide pedagogical benefits to those who were open to the lessons that could be learned. In this way "Dame Wisdom" offered herself as a gift to whoever would accept her. If experiential wisdom can be understood as the means to successful living, the acquisition of mysterious wisdom is the very goal of life.

An Intellectual Tradition

While von Rad sees this reflection on life and the experiences of life as the preoccupation of a definable class resulting in a distinguishable tradition, R.N. Whybray argues for another position. In his book, *The Intellectual Tradition in the Old Testament,* he does not assign this preoccupation with the concerns of life to a professional or esoteric group, as so many before him have done. Preferring the term "intellectual" to that of "wisdom," he regards this perspective as "a set of ideas, or an attitude to life,"[5] "and in so far as there were in every generation men who thought about [the perennial questions of life] and made their thoughts known to others, there may be said to have been an 'intellectual tradition' in Israel which was distinct from other traditions such as the historical, legal, cultic and prophetic."[6]

The distinctiveness of which he speaks is usually described in terms of what the tradition omits rather than what it contains. Unlike the other traditions, wisdom seldom if ever reflects on the events of Israel's history. Nor does it contain specifically Israelite legal, cultic, or prophetic material. Rather, attention is directed toward basic human living—how to cope with life and how to be successful in the process.

One must remember that it is the examination of the biblical texts that have led scholars to draw the conclusions that they have drawn. Such careful study cannot fail to admit the distinctiveness of some of the vocabulary, literary forms, and interests under consideration. At the same time, there is striking similarity of vocabulary, literary forms and interests in literature belonging to other biblical traditions, namely parts of Deuteronomy, some historical narratives, and prophetic material as well as certain psalms. Findings of this nature have resulted in theories of common origin of traditions, interrelatedness or significant influence of one tradition or the other. One scholar builds upon, refines or challenges the position of another. Different perspectives, different emphasis and different conclusions have resulted in the diversity of opinion on some points.

Whybray and von Rad agree on the interrelatedness of the various traditions. They disagree as to the reason for this interrelatedness. Recognizing that wisdom perceptions are found within certain historical narratives, von Rad states that wisdom "teachings did not arise from any secret doctrine but became part of the common cultural stock."[7] They would thus be incorporated into or appropriated by proponents of other traditions. Whybray, on the other hand, does not deny that Israel developed a distinctive wisdom literary tradition, but he believes that the intellectual perspective was the common ground of the total society. It did not *become* public property; it always *was* public property. It did not *become* part of the common cultural stock; it *was* part of the common cultural stock. Both men would agree that reflection on life was the common pursuit of all. They also agree that the articulation of this reflection gradually assumed a degree of distinctiveness. They disagree about the role played by this articulated reflection in the formation of tradition as well as about the existence of professional groups responsible for the preservation and further development of the tradition.

If Whybray is correct in his assessment of this intellectual tradition, then scholars must reassess the status accorded certain professional classes in ancient Israel. What role was played within this tradition by the counselor or political advisor of the king, the teacher or pedagogue, and the authors of the so-called wisdom literature? Most of Whybray's book is devoted to a careful study of vocabulary that has been traditionally associated with wisdom. It is the examination of the noun *ḥokmā* (wisdom) and the adjective *ḥākām* (wise) that led him to define wisdom as "simply a natural endowment which some persons possess in greater measure than others."[8] "It refers to innate intelligence of a quite general kind"[9] which is expressed in a variety of abilities or skills ranging from sailing a boat to advising at court. Anyone who had the necessary degree of skill required to perform a given task was considered wise. Such general designations hardly suggest a specialized group comprising the authors and trustees of true wisdom.

N B Whybray argues against a distinctive class

Differences set aside, Whybray shares many of the views of other contemporary scholars. This wisdom or, to use his own term, "intelligence" is primarily shrewdness rather than a body of knowledge to be mastered. A certain amount of it can be acquired, but even this acquisition demands innate ability and insight. Not a static possession, intelligence enables one to cope with the different situations in life as well as to take the greatest advantage of happiness that is possible. Even wisdom in the religious sense is viewed as an intellectual quality which, superior though it may be, provides full and meaningful life.

All agree that this innate or acquired intelligence will manifest itself in some manner consistent with the nature of the ability. This might be in the deft performance of some task, in the aesthetic accomplishment of artistic creation, in the cultivated habit of appropriate behavior, or in the penetrating clarity of astute advice. Because intelligence has been characteristically associated with speech, the one who knows what to say and when to say it is often considered wise. This is particularly true in societies where the spoken word assumes tremendous importance. Hence, those whose intelligence is demonstrated in the artful use of words are vouchsafed a prominent place in society. This fact may account for the conventional but inadequate view that the counselor, the teacher and the wisdom author are the official sages.

Whybray goes into great detail in discounting the theory of a professional class of sages. Addressing texts that mention the three professions of counselor, teacher and author, he concludes that while they did belong to professional groups, this does not automatically mean that they were also revered as professional sages.

It is quite clear from the biblical texts that the Israelite kings fashioned their courts after the model already present in other nations of the ancient Near Eastern world. They employed men to advise them and to administrate official royal policies. It is easy to understand how exceptional insight and the ability to use it in guiding and directing others often promised the possessor coveted prestige. A close scrutiny of relevant biblical texts prompts one to ask whether or not these texts indicate that the successful counselor was awarded the distinction "sage" while the sailor who was able to skillfully guide his bark to safe harbor was not. Whybray answers this query in the negative. He claims that only Isaiah speaks of the wisdom of the royal counselors and then in a derogatory manner. They seemed to claim superior intelligence, while the prophet upbraided them for this arrogant pretension.

Using parallels from other ancient Near Eastern societies, many scholars have written about a professional class of teachers and the establishment of schools in Israel. Whybray turns his attention to this question. No one doubts the teaching role of the priest or of the prophet. What is under consideration here is the existence of an organized system of education at the court, at the temple, or in prophetic or scribal schools. All agree that the education of youth was the responsibility of the father and, as Proverbs tells us, of the mother. When professions were hereditary the pertinent information and operating principles were also handed down within the confines of the family, perhaps an extended family. Such hereditary professions included the monarchy, the priesthood, and the scribal class. Education in these professions was an extension of family training. Whybray concludes that while great knowledge might qualify one to teach and guide others it did not thereby constitute a class of professional teachers.

Who wrote Proverbs, Job, and Qoheleth, those books traditionally referred to as Wisdom Literature? Was there perhaps a professional class of authors? Is the thinking found within these books the product of one sage? Of a small group of sages? The distillation of a common attitude or tradition? What one believes to be the provenance of the book will influence what one thinks about authorship or vice versa. If one has discounted, as Whybray has, the existence of organized schools, then the literature would not have arisen within the schools nor would it have served as textbook material for the classes. The father-son exchange found in Proverbs could well reflect the family setting, especially when the son is exhorted to listen to the admonitions of his mother as well as of his father. Job is not an official counselor or teacher. He is a once prosperous elder now dispossessed. Qoheleth is portrayed as a man of great wealth and experience. In none of these books is there a suggestion that the author belongs to or is promoting a professional class of sages. True, someone had to actually write the books. Each one of them most likely underwent several stages of redaction. These authors undoubtedly possessed keener literary ability than their contemporaries, but the intellectual tradition expressed within these works was the common store of the people.

Whybray's position can be put quite simply. Wisdom is nothing more nor less than a set of ideas, an attitude toward life. It enables one to live a life of meaning and of happiness. All can possess it in varying degrees and manifest it in diverse ways. These manifestations may be very general and indistinguishable or specialized and distinctive. While intelligence is an innate quality it can also be acquired by learning from others and from life experiences. This intelligence is not static, nor is it the exclusive domain of some official class. It grew up within the people Israel, it was articulated and manifested by the people Israel.

A Quest for Self-Understanding

James Crenshaw, in addition to making many significant creative contributions to the study of the wisdom literature of ancient Israel, has undertaken the task of editing a volume of essays on the topic entitled, *Studies in Ancient Israelite Wisdom.* He acknowledges in the Preface that "the reader may think that better essays exist on one topic or another, and that other subjects should have been covered."[10] The principle guiding his selection was "to provide a comprehensive volume on wisdom literature, with emphasis on seminal studies in English covering major areas of research."[11] A lengthy "Prolegomenon" by Crenshaw himself as well as material from one of his articles included in the volume will be examined because of their relevance to the theme under discussion.

In "Method in Determining Wisdom Influence Upon 'Historical Literature' " he sets about distinguishing between wisdom literature, wisdom tradition, and wisdom thinking. Making these distinctions he is able to underscore the importance of several different dimensions or manifestations of this reality without having to consider all of them at the same time and in the same way. Commenting on von Rad's definition, "practical knowledge of the laws of life and of the world, based on experience," he criticizes it for being so comprehensive that it is unusable. At the other end of the spectrum he places his own definition, "the quest for self-understanding in terms of relationships with things, people, and the Creator.["12] He sees this search operating on three levels: nature wisdom, practical and juridical wisdom, and theological wisdom. Making the distinctions between literature, tradition, and thinking is also consonant with the position of Whybray who, Crenshaw believes, has shown better than most that wisdom is an attitude as well as a living tradition and a body of literature.

Reiterating the principle that order lies at the heart of wisdom thinking and that this order suggests some kind of design or purpose that can and must be discerned and lived with in harmony, Crenshaw proceeds to explain the different kinds of wisdom that he perceives. First among these is nature wisdom. In order to simply survive, women and men must be able to master or co-exist with the natural world. Observation of the world and its movement have resulted in the recognition of a certain amount of regularity within its operations and similarity among the characteristics of its natural phenomena. Lists known as onomastica, the precursors of the physical sciences, were humankind's attempt to conquer the universe or at least not be conquered by it.

Both practical and juridical wisdom resulted from reflection upon evaluation of the consequences of social interaction. Peace and harmony could only exist where social order was maintained. Whatever manner of behavior resulted in happiness or guaranteed the status quo was pursued; whatever threatened it was avoided. This aspect of wisdom thinking gave rise to the theory of retribution that stated that the wise will be rewarded with peace and security while the fool will suffer the consequences of foolishness.

The fourth kind of wisdom touches the question of theodicy, the vindication of the justice of God. If indeed order lies at the heart of wisdom, how is one to explain the pervading injustice or disorder in the world? The manner in which this question is answered will determine the nature of the relationship between humankind and the Creator.

These four kinds of wisdom (nature, practical and juridical, and theological) constitute what Crenshaw calls "self-understanding in terms of relationships with things, people, and the Creator."

A final distinction that Crenshaw makes is between family or clan wisdom, court wisdom, and scribal wisdom. The first type he would identify with the "common cultural stock." Here he is closer to Whybray with his notion of the intellectual tradition than to von Rad who views this common stock as a literary expression. However, he is in stark disagreement with Whybray when he speaks of professional groups responsible for the transmission of this wisdom to others.

Returning to the distinction made above, Crenshaw believes that family wisdom aims at developing the skills needed for the mastery of life. The elders exhorted proper behavior that would engender wise living and subsequent happiness. Court wisdom, on the other hand, was not satisfied with exhortation. It was intended to teach worldly manners to those select few destined to rule. Scribal wisdom was universal, endeavoring to instill religious dogmas in all. The method employed here was dialogic and admonitory.

Judging von Rad's definition of wisdom too comprehensive and Whybray's too ambiguous, Crenshaw has arrived at a many nuanced definition that is far-reaching in scope, but replete with distinctions that allow him to be very specific in his focus.

Building on Walter Zimmerli's statement, "Wisdom thinks resolutely within a framework of a theology of creation. Its theology is creation theology,"[13] Crenshaw attempts to break new ground in showing the relationship between creation and retribution. He does not subscribe to von Rad's principle that *Heilsgeschichte,* salvation history, is the basic framework of ancient Israelite thought. He agrees with those who hold that creation is the dominant theme within which all other views move, and he has come to this position from his investigation of the ancient Near East's preoccupation with world order. If this theme was the dominant structure of thought, then order and its opposite (chaos) were primary concerns of the faith of Israel and were not merely peripheral ideas. From this perspective Crenshaw develops three points: the order established at the time of creation is constantly threatened by the forces of chaos; this threat raises the question of theodicy (the justice of God in allowing chaos to hold sway) to which creation provides an answer; if creation is the defense of divine justice, creation theology is concerned with the integrity of God.

The first point is comprised of a presupposition of faith and an observation of fact. It is obvious that order is under constant assault.

The disintegration of international and national harmony, the antagonism between and within social groups, and the personal struggles that go to make up each and every life are examples of this. While there is no empirical evidence proving the validity of the presupposition of faith, there can be no doubt that the ancient Near Eastern world, Israel included, believed in the primordial establishment of order in the universe.

Within the literary corpus of Israel, the Book of Job plays a significant role in raising the question of theodicy. Presuming that order has indeed been established, how does one explain the prevalence of chaos? Throughout the book, the justice of God and the order within creation are frequently juxtaposed. The Yahweh speeches are superb in the way they bring Job and the reader to acknowledge the wisdom and power of the Creator. Using one of the very principles of wisdom pedagogy—"learn from nature"—they bring Job to his knees in humble acceptance. Just as nature teaches the existence of order and regularity, so it reveals marvels too mysterious for the human mind to comprehend. Creation with its unfathomable mysteries is a defense of the mighty Creator who cannot be limited by human standards of justice.

Crenshaw concludes his argument by placing creation under the rubric of justice. He states that "the function of creation theology is to undergird the belief in divine justice" which he calls "the fundamental question of human existence, namely, the integrity of God."[14] Creation and justice are intimately connected both in regard to the primordial creation and in the continual victory of order over chaos within each person and within society as a whole.

An Effort To Establish Order

Israelite Wisdom, the volume of essays in honor of Samuel Terrien, consists of six major sections each focusing on one major aspect of wisdom research. The second section, "On the Meaning and Study of Israelite Wisdom," includes an article by Roland Murphy, O. Carm. entitled "Wisdom—Thesis and Hypothesis." One of the positions that he espouses is a challenge of the thesis that "biblical wisdom issues from the effort to discover order in human life."[15] This article, along with an earlier one which appeared in another publication,[16] sets forth Murphy's perspective on the theme under consideration here.

The influence exerted upon Israel by other Near Eastern cultures cannot be denied. This influence would include thought patterns and possibly literary expression. The teaching about Ma'at has been summarized above. Murphy believes that the contemporary view concerning Israel's perception of cosmic order has resulted from an exaggerated interpretation of parallelism with this Egyptian doctrine. He challenges this view by refuting arguments based on apparent correspondence between the natural and the social orders, the influence of one order upon the other, and the question of retribution.

An examination of the literature shows that the texts are concerned with human conduct, not with the natural order. When these two orders are juxtaposed it is for the sake of comparison. Human conduct and the natural order seem to illustrate each other. To suggest that Israel moved from the recognition of similarity, of which the biblical texts provide ample evidence, to the postulation of an all-encompassing principle of order, is a step that Murphy is not prepared to take.

He does not deny the prominence of the theme of a conflict between world order and chaos. This theme appears throughout the Hebrew Scriptures. He questions whether or not ancient Israelites perceived human conduct as impinging upon this order.

When he turns to the theory of retribution he qualifies his stand. Israel did recognize justice as a given order. The righteous would be rewarded and the wicked punished. However, this is not a thesis springing primarily nor exclusively from the wisdom tradition. It flows naturally from covenantal commitment and is part of the fabric of prophetic and Deuteronomic theology. Nor does this theory exclude the freedom of Yahweh, as wisdom determinism tends to do. It is this latter point that lies at the heart of Murphy's objection to the theory of strict world order. The Scriptures insist again and again on Yahweh's freedom.

Even if the world order is the product of the wisdom and power of the Creator, does its existence not mean that all are subject to it, including the Creator? Is this view not basic to the demands that Job makes upon God? God is obliged to comply with the necessity of world order. Or is God free of such constraints and apparently capricious, as Job alleges? Murphy claims that Israel cannot cling tenaciously to faith in a God who acts freely and at the same time hold a rigid view of cosmic order. Though he feels compelled to speak of order, even von Rad admits the conflict between the notion of order and that of divine freedom.[17]

Murphy would reword the thesis to read, "Biblical wisdom issues from the effort to *put* order in human life." This perspective seriously alters the view of world order, but then so does faith in the freedom of God. It also challenges the claim made by Whybray and others that world order is the basic construct of ancient Near Eastern thought. This challenge need not be total rejection. Rather than state that God is experienced within the context of established order, one could say that the experience is within the context of the *search* for order. Murphy suggests that "one would do better to speak of human's imposing an order (however provisory) upon the chaotic experiences of life, by analysis and classification."[18] Would not this make chaos the basic construct?

Among many other statements made within the article, two are relevant to this chapter. Murphy has a brief discussion of the major interpretations of the personification of wisdom. Calling von Rad's theory of " 'meaning' implanted by God in creation" a daring move, he admits that, though it is still an hypothesis, there is enough evidence in the text to support his view.

He is also in sympathy with Whybray's idea of an intellectual tradition in ancient Israel. He too believes that the wisdom mentality was much broader than the literature that has survived. He disagrees with Whybray, however, in the latter's denial of a professional class of sages.

Every definition not only reveals the identity of the reality under consideration but also distinguishes it from what it is not. That which differentiates also limits. The specific study of the phenomenon known as wisdom and of various definitions of this phenomenon would be incomplete and the view severely distorted if a serious investigative look were not directed toward the question of limitations. These limitations exist on several levels.

Coping with Reality

Lest one be left with the impression that von Rad's view of order is rather simplistic, a perusal of his chapter on "Limits of Wisdom"[19] will bring to light his concise articulation of the tension that exists between what he calls sacral order and the worldly domain. Ancient patriarchal-sacral orders provided the Israelite with the security of knowing that the significant and memorable events of history were the result of Yahweh's activity in the national affairs of the people. Such a world view is behind much of the literary tradition of Israel and finds its articulation in the credal statements which summarize this *Heilsgeschichte* or salvation history. The wisdom movement, on the other hand, accorded more value to human endeavor and enterprise and thus contributed to a desacralization of history and a secularization of the world. Wisdom focused not so much on divine activity and accomplishment but on that of women and men. This led to a rethinking of long-accepted ideas. The manner in which these two perspectives, viz., sacral orders and worldly domain, were balanced varied in response to different historical times, the experiences of the people and their theological points of view. They never relinquished their faith in God's free activity in their lives, but they seemed at times to move toward a radical secularization according to which God was restrained by the orders of the world. Some writings emphasize one aspect of this dilemma itself as evidence of the limits of wisdom in explaining Israel's perception of reality and life.

Basic to wisdom understanding is the thesis that one can learn from experience because certain consequences are inherent in the act itself. This led to the prediction of underlying principles or laws of order. However, experience also taught that life is unpredictable. Regardless of how attentive one is to principles and values there is much that is beyond human calculation and control. Nor can one designate which experiences of life are predictable and which unpredictable. What appeared to be obvious and dependable at one time and in one circumstance was uncertain and unstable at another. In the chapter entitled "The Doctrine of the Proper Time" von Rad addresses this point: ". . . in the experiences of the world in which men find themselves nothing of absolute validity can be affirmed.

What is experienced at any given occasion has always shown itself to
be in some way conditioned and relative."[20] If this is the case,
wisdom cannot provide a format to be followed that will guarantee
pre-determined results. To understand wisdom in this way is really
to misunderstand it. Wisdom is not a body of experiential knowledge
to be mastered and applied in situations of life, but the flexibility of
mind that assists one in discerning the right time and the fitting place
for the appropriate behavior.

These nuances do not deny the theory or order; they modify it.
Rather than viewing order in terms of rigid determinism, one must
allow for a degree of conditioned relativity. Even this perspective is
incapable of answering the challenge of Qoheleth (Ecclesiastes) who
claims that it is no consolation knowing that everything has its
proper time (cf. 3:1–8) if the Almighty withholds knowledge of this
time. Here one sees the limitations of wisdom quite clearly. Only
God knows the proper times. Human experience and personal reflection on the regularity within nature are incapable of supplying this
knowledge. Women and men reach a point in their search for this
wisdom and are frustrated with the inadequacy of their acquisition.

In Chapter VII, "The Essentials for Coping with Reality," von
Rad develops the act-consequence relationship. He states that "one
of the main tasks which the wise men, in their search for knowledge,
took upon themselves was the mastering of the 'contingent.'" By
"contingent" he means those events which cannot be understood
purely on the basis of the familiar. He claims that a basic human
urge is to limit the sphere of contingency and to seize upon some
element of meaning in the contingent event regardless of how hidden. This throws into question the theory of an unyielding order
behind the succession of events. Experience shows that "nothing, no
human behaviour, no experience, no value can be recorded as being
completely unambiguous."[21] Wisdom does not enable one to tran-
scend the ambiguous, but to deal with it appropriately. Neither
contingency nor ambiguity need undermine a versatile theory of
order. On the contrary, they may be merely indications of the
limitations of human wisdom. There is indeed a cosmic order but the
human mind cannot grasp all of its ramifications, even those which
impinge upon human experience.

The question of the unpredictability of events is also treated by von Rad in the chapter with which this discussion began, "Limits of Wisdom." There he attempts to reconcile the dilemma between the sacral orders and the worldly domain. Between the human plan and its execution many things can happen. It is precisely here that divine action can intervene. While the initiative may be human, the accomplishment is not. This idea is expressed in the contemporary adage, "Man proposes; God disposes." This point of view does not exonerate women and men from taking hold of life and living it. It presumes this and demands much more. One must be ever open to the activity of God and resist the temptation of resting in false security. The fact that one's plans have achieved the desired goal is no guarantee that life has been mastered and wisdom attained. It should be interpreted as the graciousness of God who brought the action to completion. Both God and the human agent participated in the event, but in different ways and to different degrees. What is between human intentions and the actual realization is unpredictability, not determinism. The format is the special domain of Yahweh and calls for trust in God on the part of the human. Thus Israel could say, "The fear of the Lord is the beginning of wisdom" (Prov 1:7; 9:10; 15:33; Ps 111:10; Jb 28:28). Cognizant of the importance of mastering the rules of life, the women and men of wisdom knew that life "is determined not by rules but by God."[22]

It is at this point of his discussion that von Rad questions the accuracy of the use of the term "order": "Can one really say that the teachers were searching for a world order? Our findings, especially our discussion of the Yahweh proverbs, suggested, rather, that one can in no way speak of a world order as really existing between God and man."[23] As von Rad sees it, ancient Israel struggled in a world of contingency and ambiguity, at times discerning inherent laws and limited spheres of order, but always being called to the possibility of an encounter with the incommensurable God.

The purpose of this chapter has not been to pit one scholar against another, but to give examples of the complexity of the matter under scrutiny and of the diversity of scholarly opinion regarding this matter. Everyone has the same starting point, viz., the biblical text. Each has an individual perspective and emphasis, not to mention presuppositions.

2
Setting

Israel's wisdom or intellectual tradition did not develop in a vacuum. It was part of a much broader movement within the ancient Near Eastern world. Reference to the sages of these foreign nations can be found within the biblical text itself, usually within passages which portray an Israelite outstripping a non-Israelite in wisdom. Joseph succeeded in interpreting Pharaoh's dream even when the magicians and sages of Egypt failed (cf. Gen 41:8). Job had a reputation which surpassed that of all of the people of the East (cf. Jb 1:3). Such allusions to the existence of an international wisdom movement were substantiated when, in the beginning of the twentieth century, extensive non-Israelite literary evidence came to light. Examples from Egyptian, Mesopotamian and Canaanite texts reveal remarkable similarity with some of the biblical material. There is common subject matter, the literary forms are similar and the world view corresponds with that of Israel. Lest one think, as some have thought in the past, that Israel was the forerunner and the others followed its lead in this movement, study has shown that these non-Israelite texts are significantly older than comparable biblical material. More likely than not, Israel borrowed from its neighbors and adapted and reinterpreted when necessary. Specialists of Egyptian and Babylonian literature refrain from calling this material "wisdom" because within these cultures "wisdom" is akin to skill in cult and magic. They prefer the designation "instruction."

Instruction from Egypt and Mesopotamia

This literature can be conveniently divided into two major categories: traditional and speculative. The first type focuses on the practical and moral lessons learned from experience. The second is a challenge to principles which have developed from these lessons but which appear to be inadequate in expressing the meaning of life. Much of the literature of Egypt falls under the first category and has the special title "teaching." Notable examples of this type include: *Instruction of Ptah-hotep,* an Egyptian vizier; *Instruction for Meri-kare* written for the prospective pharaoh by his father; *Instruction of Ani,* a scribe with minor official status; *Instruction of Amenemope,* another royal official. Each of these instructions is closely associated with the court. Two points should be recalled: the Egyptian concept of Ma'at, divine cosmic order, and the affinity that the ancients believed to exist between divinity and royalty. Hence, it is easy to understand how they associated wisdom or its equivalent with both the gods and the monarchy. According to their belief, wisdom was the originator and guarantor of cosmic order and the king possessed divine attributes, one of which was cosmic power. Therefore, the political order for which the king was responsible would be safe-guarded through the instrumentality of the same cosmic power. The status quo was divinely ordained and sustained and human behavior must conform to it. Those responsible for maintaining order must be trained in proper procedure. It appears that this instruction was for the officials of the court. It was not until social upheaval forced Egypt to re-examine its traditional teachings that a more pessimistic but at the same time universal literature gained prominence.

When society is somewhat stable its teaching is directed toward ensuring this stability. When the fabric of society begins to unravel, women and men challenge empty directives of the past and wrestle with the weighty questions of meaning and of life. This struggle is reflected in Egyptian literature. The *Dispute Over Suicide* shows a man in the throes of this struggle. The *Song of the Harper* admits the fleetingness of happiness and counsels enjoyment while it lasts. These are two examples of literature that has been called speculative, protest, skeptical or pessimistic.

In addition to our knowledge of Egyptian literature, recent scholarship has provided examples of Mesopotamian counterparts. Although the material is arranged somewhat differently, the literary forms are similar to those appearing in Egyptian texts. The most significant example of this is a work entitled *Counsels of Wisdom* which is probably a collection of moral exhortations of a ruler for his son. The *Story of Ahiqar* and the *Story of the Three Youths* is incorporated into 1 Esdras 3:1—5:6.

Mesopotamia also struggled with the uncertainties of life and preserved pieces of literature which record that struggle. "I Will Praise the Lord of Wisdom" has often been called the *Babylonian Job* or *Pilgrim's Progress* because of the similarity it bears to these works. The *Dialogue About Human Misery* and the *Dialogue of Pessimism* are both concerned with what appears to be the lack of justice in life.

The Mesopotamian texts also provide evidence of the existence of a scribal school in ancient Sumer called *e-dubba* or "house of tablets." Because of the correspondence of the literature some have drawn the conclusion that Israel, like Mesopotamia, had established scribal schools. They would also say that, like Egypt which held a belief in Ma'at or cosmic order, Israel perceived order as the dominant structure of the world. We have already discussed contemporary scholarly opinions on these points. While they may differ as to the extent and degree of influence exerted by these nations, they do agree that Israel's wisdom literature attests to this influence.

Examination of the texts from the ancient Near Eastern world provides ample evidence of the connection between didactic literature and the monarchy. Was there a comparable relationship in Israel or have writers selected passages from the biblical text to support a contrived theory that such a relationship did exist? How historically accurate is the popular tradition of Solomonic enlightenment and the unsurpassed wisdom of Solomon himself? Once again scholarship has provided a variety of answers to our questions.

Wisdom and the Court

It is clear that Gerhard von Rad believes that the court was one of the chief centers of didactic tradition. His examination of the Book of Proverbs has brought him to this conclusion. He holds that the references to the functions of the courtiers suggest that the Israelite monarchy was patterned after that of its neighbors. As in Egypt, officials were expected to have mastered diplomatic niceties of speech which would put them in good stead while on political missions. The court also had its contingent of astrologers and interpreters of dreams. Even though most of the proverbs had very little to do with the court but were concerned with day to day living, von Rad still insisted that the royal sages were responsible for the collection and transmission of the didactic material. He believed that "the king was the foremost champion and promoter of all searching after wisdom."[24] One must turn to some of his earlier writing to find his position on the possibility of Solomonic enlightenment.

In his essay "The Form-Critical Problem of the Hexateuch" written as early as 1938, von Rad puts forth his view of the radical change which took place in the thinking of Israel with the coming of the monarchy.[25] According to him, pre-monarchical Israel perceived its encounters with Yahweh in sacral terms. The cultus was the shaper of old traditions and the locus of new ones. The enlightenment of the monarchy changed this. "The main emphasis of God's dealings with his people is now to be sought outside the sacral institutions."[26] This is a new point of view for Israel. It does not deny the reality of God's activity in the lives of the people. Rather, it is a new and revolutionary way of understanding it. No longer are the most significant events those attributed to divine action exclusively. Recognition of and appreciation for human accomplishment begins to exert pressure on the religious and literary consciousness of the nation. Von Rad highlights several biblical units as proof of this new understanding: the Yahwist's interpretation of the early historical traditions; the Joseph narrative (Gen 37—50); the succession narrative (2 Sam 9—1 Kgs 2). Each of these units portrays divine power active in ordinary human events. These are stories of human affairs, not divine interventions. This is especially true of the succession

narrative where only three instances of a divine critique can be found
(cf. 2 Sam 11:27; 12:24; 17:14). There is no doubting that there was a
startling redirection of Israel's perspective. Von Rad claims that
there is clear literary evidence of it.

A second and more recent article by von Rad reiterates his
views on the role played by the monarchy in this redirection of
perspective. He describes the period of the early monarchy as one "of
'enlightenment,' an awakening of spiritual self-consciousness."[27] The
patriarchal traditions had ceased to play a formative role in the life
of the nation and had been relegated to cultic remembrance. There
was a newly awakened interest in spiritual and rational powers as
well as in natural history. Proverbs that speak of the wisdom of the
heart (cf. Prov 10:8) illustrate the former while the onomasticon or
word list is an example of the latter. Both of these concerns appear in
a wisdom or intellectual or didactic movement. Von Rad concludes
that this movement arose and took hold during the early monarchy.

Was it the monarchy with its modeling after neighboring cultures that brought on this "enlightenment" or had it already begun
imperceptively and merely been brought to maturity under the
patronage of the king? Von Rad would say that there probably were
proverbial reflections current in Israel long before the monarchy.
This popular wisdom was preserved at locations other than the court
but was eventually gathered by royal sages into the literary units that
have survived. Walter Brueggemann has done a considerable amount
of work on this topic.[28] He gives substantial credit to the king,
especially David, for having effected the "enlightenment" and to the
court writers, especially the Yahwist, for having preserved the traditions and having given them a Davidic and further theological
interpretation.

Wisdom of the People

James Crenshaw has been quite critical of the above position.[29]
He has done an extensive review of *Wisdom in Israel*[30] as well as
written his own book on von Rad's thought.[31] He does not believe
that the Solomonic period was as revolutionary as the above writers
contend. Solomon may very well have introduced foreign elements

into his court, but one should not draw the conclusion that Israel was ignorant of a humanistic perspective prior to this move nor that the sacral view of life subsequently vanished. The traditions about Solomon's wisdom are legendary in character as a closer look behind them will show. It is clear that Solomon the "wise" administrator was responsible for the secession of the northern tribes (cf. 1 Kgs 11—12). Secondly, Solomonic attribution of some collections in the Book of Proverbs is a late editorial contrivance. Crenshaw claims that there is no hard evidence for believing that there was an "enlightenment." Those who insist that there was such a movement have based their claim on what is known of the Egyptian court and have drawn Israelite parallels where the amount of evidence does not warrant it. This does not deny Solomonic patronage of national desacralization of traditions and a resultant secularization, though it does challenge the hypothesis of a royal initiator of and force behind the wisdom movement.

Crenshaw continues, "A corollary of belief in the existence of an active wisdom movement under Solomon's sponsorship is the emergence of a class ethic."[32] He is referring to an ethical standard for the upper class. Even a cursory view of Proverbs will reveal that very few proverbs apply merely to the court. Most of them address ordinary life situations. Crenshaw concludes from this that the proverbs were directed to different classes of people: the family, the court and the school. He proposes that maxims originating in the clan and counseling self-mastery could have been quite easily carried over into a royal or scribal setting. In this he agrees with von Rad who emphasizes the importance of the court but recognizes the popular wisdom as well. von Rad believes that this clan wisdom was collected, preserved and transmitted by royal sages. Crenshaw judges that the information pertaining to those responsible for the literature is too obscure to make any definite statements about them at this time.

Wisdom and Israelite Revival

Studies in Israelite Wisdom includes an insightful article by R.B.Y. Scott, "Solomon and the Beginnings of Wisdom," wherein the author investigates the connection of Solomon with the Israelite wisdom movement and the literature that grew out of it. According to him, the theory of such a connection rests upon two biblical sections: the narratives about the king's wisdom in 1 Kings 5:9–14; 10:1–10, 13, 23–24, and the superscriptions to the collections in Proverbs 1:1; 10:1; 25:1.

Scott begins by affirming the historicity of some fundamental association of Solomon with wisdom. His involvement in the movement may have been profoundly exaggerated as the tradition was transmitted, but the basic fact remains rooted in history. However, the wisdom for which Solomon is praised in 1 Kings is knowledge of the natural world, not insight into human behavior as is the focus in the Book of Proverbs. One type of knowledge is no guarantee of expertise in the other. These are two different traditions and will be analyzed separately.

Before discussing the highlights of Scott's article a word should be said about a second article on this topic. It appears immediately after Scott's in the same collection of essays.[33] Written by Albrecht Alt, "Solomonic Wisdom" first appeared in 1951. It is a treatment of the subject matter of Solomon's wisdom. Alt points out that the biblical description of the king's knowledge corresponds to the onomasticon which has been found in the texts of ancient Egypt, Canaan and Mesopotamia. The data indicates that the form appeared in Babylon before its counterpart emerged in Egypt. He suggests that Solomon was influenced by this type of wisdom but that the Israelite king was innovative in his use of it. It was this creativity that earned for him the reputation of a wisdom that superseded all those who had preceded him.

Returning to Scott, he points out that Solomon's wisdom is defined in the three passages from 1 Kings as intellectual superiority and universal knowledge. In the two passages from chapter 10, the great wealth of the king is the natural counterpart to his wisdom. There is no question as to the extent of Solomon's riches. He launched extensive building projects including the temple, numerous palaces and chariot cities. It was the burdensome policy of taxation for revenue to pay for these royal enterprises that precipitated the revolt of the northern tribes. In spite of the disastrous consequences of his program of aggrandizement, Solomon's building projects continue to attest to his glory even to this day. Scott suggests that,

contrary to popular legend which believes that Solomon's wisdom
was the source of his prosperity, it was because of his great wealth
and the manner in which he patterned his reign after that of neighboring monarchs that Solomon was considered a king like the kings
of the nations (cf. 2 Sam 8:5–18). This royal image included incom-
parable wisdom and, for Israel's king, wisdom which outstripped
that of his contemporaries.

Scott further asserts that the passages that glorify Solomon are
interpolations of the tradition. The underlying theology of these
narratives is Deuteronomic. Within this tradition royal wisdom
included: the ability to rule successfully; the insight to distinguish
right from wrong as a judge would render true justice; intellectual
brilliance and encyclopedic knowledge. The legends about Solomon
could have easily developed from ideas found in the Deuteronomic
editor's composition of Yahweh's promise to Solomon which were
communicated in the dream recorded in 1 Kings 3:5–13. Scott's
interpretation of these texts acknowledges Solomonic prominence in
the establishment of Near Eastern royal structures and policies in
ancient Israel without attributing to Solomon instigation of an intellectual revolution that catapulted the nation into a non-sacral or
secularized world view and that produced a body of literature which
testified to this revolution. It does not answer the question of the
origin of Israel's wisdom nor does it account for the legendary
Solomonic tradition.

Scott proceeds with his analysis by turning to the titles of the
collection in Proverbs. The third superscription (25:1) mentions the
men of Hezekiah. Here is solid evidence that there existed an organized literary wisdom movement associated with the monarchy, but
it was during the eighth century, considerably later than Solomon.
To suggest that there was not an organized movement before this
time does not deny the existence of an earlier popular gnomic
tradition (cf. 1 Sam 10:12; 2 Sam 14:2; etc.), but there is no biblical
evidence that there was a school of literary wisdom earlier. It
appears that Hezekiah attempted national revival and reform. The
Chronicler credits him with cleansing the temple and restoring the
liturgy and thereby compares his concerns with those of his illustri-
ous predecessor Solomon (cf. 1 Chr 29—30). This tradition, though
also a post-exilic interpretation, most likely reflects Hezekiah's at-

tempt to model his reign after that of Solomon. Additional grounds
for this view appear in the Book of Isaiah.[34] There existed at this time
strong Egyptian political and cultural influence in the court of
Hezekiah. Like Solomon, this king put great trust in horses and
chariots and the symbol of power and glory that they created. In
addition to this, organized wisdom enjoyed great influence at court.
Unlike the period of Solomon when wisdom was the prerogative of
the king, during Hezekiah's reign there was a group of professional
sages. Isaiah was in frequent conflict with them over their pro-
Egyptian political policy.

Hezekiah's revival included religious reform, political and eco-
nomic expansion and literary development. "It is the most probable
time for the bringing together of the northern and southern historical
traditions, prophetic records and psalm collections."[35] These projects
were probably accomplished by the "men of Hezekiah," members of
the scribal school. Scott suggests that it was this scribal school that
affixed to Solomon's reputation as a successful ruler the added
tribute of first-rate sage. Hence, Hezekiah's modeling of Solomon's
administrative policies opened the way for the emergence of a Solomonic legend wherein the sophistication that was present at the time
of Hezekiah was ascribed to the earlier period in order to enhance
the tradition about Solomon's wisdom.

Wisdom and Law

One point remains to be discussed and that is the actual socio-
logical setting of the origin of the wisdom tradition. Both Crenshaw
in his "Prolegomenon"[36] and Murphy in "Wisdom—Thesis and
Hypothesis"[37] mention new emphases that have been brought to the
investigation by the studies of other authors. Because they agree with
the findings of these works but do not give their readers much
indication as to the content of the studies, it might be helpful for
those who are unfamiliar with the studies to be introduced to them.
A few words about four of these works seem in order. All of them
concentrate on the relationship of wisdom with law.

After studying the form and content of the motive clause that
forms part of the Israelite law statement, Berend Gemser concluded
that the proverbial wisdom that is found within the legal form might

be very ancient and not a later addition as had been held earlier.[38] J.P. Audet took these findings one step further.[39] He claimed that ultimately all law structure and authority was derived from the family. This led to an investigation of the origins of wisdom which he traced back to the family unit. A study of the prohibitions in the laws in the Hebrew Scriptures led Erhard Gerstenberger to a comparison of these prohibitions with the admonitions found within wisdom lore.[40] The parallels that he discovered convinced him that the family was the locus of such authority. Wolfgang Richter concurred with these findings and went on to propose a second setting for original wisdom thinking, the school.[41] It seems that many contemporary writers have followed the lead of these and other scholars believing that wisdom originated in the family and not at court as a result of an influx of foreign culture. The monarchy was undoubtedly the source of some of the tradition, but the view of its importance has been significantly modified in recent years.

3
Proverbs

The Book of Proverbs has enjoyed a place of prominence and respectability in both the Hebrew and the Christian traditions. Unlike Ben Sirach and the Wisdom of Solomon, its inspirational authoritativeness has not been questioned nor has its theological message been debated, as is the case with Job and Qoheleth. Where opinions about the book do differ, they are less concerned with theological meanings and arguments than with questions about the setting in life out of which the individual sayings as well as the wisdom movement itself developed—a theme already discussed in earlier pages of this study—and the compilation and final editing of the book.

All agree that Proverbs is an anthology of sorts, thus lacking any suggestion of narrative style. A casual glance at the content reveals that it is composed of various collections of sayings each having its own title:

1:1	The Proverbs of Solomon
10:1	The Proverbs of Solomon
22:17	The Sayings of the Wise
24:23	The Sayings of the Wise
25:1	The Proverbs of Solomon

29

30:1   The Words of Agur

31:1   The Words of Lemuel

Content suggests that even within these collections there are individual units retaining their own identity. An example of this is the poem extolling the qualities of the ideal wife (31:10–31).

In addition to a specific superscription, some of the collections also exhibit unique stylistic features. The first collection (1—9) is composed of individual sayings so arranged as to result in a short essay about a particular theme. The tone here is religious and the phrase "fear of the Lord" seems to be the prominent theme. Within this collection one finds the classic description of personified wisdom which is understood as closely associated with the deity and present at the creation of the universe (8:22ff). It has been said that all of the major themes of the book appear initially in this first collection which thus serves as a kind of prologue for the rest of the book. If this is true, there is a literary link between this first collection and the editing of the entire book, a point to be taken up later.

The second collection (10—22:16) could well be subdivided according to differences in proverbial form. Chapters 10—15 consist of proverbs in antithetic parallelism while the remaining chapters are not consistent in form. A description of the different parallel forms will follow later. Here attention is given to the overall composition of the book.

A great deal has been written about the correspondence between the third collection (22:17—24:22) and the *Instruction of Amenemope*. Unlike the material that precedes it, this section exhibits little if any parallelism. Rather, it resembles the style of the Egyptian work, even adapting its pattern of thirty chapters.

The fourth collection (25—29) resembles the second in its preference for antithetic parallelism. It also utilizes a form of comparison. An examination of the minor collections (30 and 31) reveals their miscellaneous character. Such a description does not deny the internal coherence of the individual pieces, but indicates that the chapters are not units in themselves.

Since this biblical book is regarded here as a collection of proverbs, it might be well to attempt a definition of the word proverb itself. The Hebrew word *mashal* is usually translated as "comparison" or "similitude." It is a wise saying, i.e., one that illuminates hidden truth by comparing it with something already known. As a saying it can take several forms: the simple statement of experiential fact; a statement of comparison or contrast; a riddle, an allegory or a taunt; etc. It appears in the form of a simple maxim or of a more complicated sentence. Its purpose is didactic and it is often expressed as exhortation or admonition.

Since the primary purpose of wisdom is to point toward and ensure enjoyment of the good life, the themes that comprise wisdom thought give evidence of this concern. The Book of Proverbs teaches the wisdom ideology by contrasting opposites such as the wise and the foolish, goodness and folly, justice and wickedness. This contrast extends to the personification of Dame Wisdom and Dame Folly and the specific paths or manners of behavior that lead to each. These, along with the maxim "fear of the Lord," are the predominant themes of the Book of Proverbs.

This Solomonic book has been both praised and decried—praised as an anthology of the experiential wisdom of ancient Israel replete with artistic expressions of truth, and decried as a collection of propagandist instruction intended to endorse and ensure the status quo. It has been quoted in support of quite diverse and sometimes opposing styles of behavior. Each of these interpretations of the biblical material is perhaps valid yet always incomplete without the other. The intellectual and literary achievement demonstrated in this book would truly be minimized if the perception of truth that it expresses were not appreciated in its specificity. A simple adage can hardly express the totality of truth. It can only articulate a limited perspective. Hence a collection of such articulations results in a portrait that is impressionistic rather than photographic.

The Literary Form

A closer look at the proverb as a literary form will assist one in appreciating the role it played in Israel's intellectual tradition. Von Rad goes into great detail in explaining "The Forms in Which

Knowledge Is Expressed."[42] He begins by impressing upon the reader the prominence of poetry in Israel's teaching. This means more than poetic expression. It implies poetic perception as well. The modern world of science and technology scarcely appreciates the aesthetic point of view of the ancients because of its own insistence on the language of the so-called exact sciences. Its designation of ancient concepts as "pre-scientific" or "pre-critical" betrays its disparaging attitude, and this to its own loss. Ancient Israel's intensive encounter with reality was aesthetic and could be adequately expressed only in artistic thought patterns and literary forms.

The ancient world expressed its insights into and reflections upon life in short pithy adages. The settings out of which these sayings grew were discussed in the previous chapter. Acknowledging the existence and importance of folk wisdom and popular proverbs, von Rad turns his attention to an analysis of the structure of the literary proverbs which, according to him, came from the schools. This epigrammatic poetry comprises most of the Book of Proverbs.

Fundamental to the structure of poetic forms in the ancient Near East is a kind of parallelism described as "thought rhyme," wherein the poet expresses an idea from two different perspectives. After having articulated the first point of view, the poet had countless possibilities for the second expression. The fund of insight from human experience was inexhaustible. "What is being aimed at is not precision in the concepts, but precision in the reproduction of the subject-matter, if possible over the whole range."[43]

The single line was probably the basic form of ancient Israelite poetry. The simplest form of parallelism is called synonymous. In it, the two parts say more or less the same thing, the second merely repeating the first with a slight variation. Examples of this type include:

> I have taught you the way of wisdom;
> > I have led you in the paths of uprightness.

> > > > Prov 4:11

> My fruit is better than gold, even fine gold,
> > and my yield than choice silver.

> > > > Prov 8:19

A second type is the antithetic parallelism wherein contrasts are juxtaposed. These are contrasts but not precise opposites and ultimately they say the same thing.

> The memory of the righteous is a blessing,
>   but the name of the wicked will rot.
>
> Prov 10:7

> The tongue of the righteous is choice silver;
>   The mind of the wicked is of little worth.
>
> Prov 10:20

Because synonymous parallelism does not demand exact equivalence and antithetic parallelism does not require precise contrast, the second part of each of these poetic lines can be drawn from a wide variety of possibilities. The result is a collection of sayings which are remarkable for their accuracy of insight and fluidity of expression. The third type of parallelism is called synthetic. The second part of this saying neither repeats nor contrasts the idea of the first part. Instead, there is a development of thought. The second part advances the statement of the first and moves toward a new thought.

> The beginning of strife is like letting out water;
>   so quit before the quarrel breaks out.
>
> Prov 17:14

> If a king judges the poor with equity
>   his throne will be established forever.
>
> Prov 29:14

Von Rad claims that popular proverbs do not occur in this parallel structure. They lack the kind of development and refinement found within this didactic poetry which, as stated earlier, he associates with the schools.

To describe this material as didactic is not to imply that all proverbial teaching is admonitory. While it is true that one of the major focuses of this tradition is exhortation to appropriate behavior, its primary interest is the recording of human perceptions. These, once learned, could expand one's understanding of life and of the world. All of this contributed to the humanizing of women and men. The Book of Proverbs contains several forms of didactic poetry and all possess unmistakable pedagogical value.

Numerical sayings are a listing of very dissimilar items which do possess one surprising element of similarity. These sayings perform the same function as do riddles, challenging one's insight and ability to discern hidden likenesses.

> Three things are never satisfied;
>> four never say, "Enough":
> Sheol, the barren womb, the earth ever thirsty for water,
>> and the fire which never says, "Enough."
>>>> Prov 30:15b–16

Another example of a teaching tool is autobiographical stylization. In it a personal discovery is recounted in order to draw out a lesson.

> I passed by the field of a sluggard,
>> by the vineyard of a man without sense;
> And lo, it was all overgrown with thorns;
>> the ground was covered with nettles,
>> and its stone wall was broken down.
> Then I saw and considered it;
>> I looked and received instruction.
>>>> Prov 24:30–32

Although this does suggest a lesson in responsibility, it is not admonition in the strict sense. These are but a few of the literary forms treated by von Rad. Other forms enjoy more prominent roles in different biblical books and will be mentioned when those books are discussed. From this brief survey one can see von Rad's agreement with those who hold that Proverbs does contain expressions of Israel's experiential wisdom.

Ethical Instruction

In the chapter entitled "The Significance of Orders for Correct Social Behaviour" he treats the question of rules of conduct and the role they played in the social life of the nation. Departing from the practice of placing "wisdom" under the heading of "ethics," von Rad doubts whether one can correctly use the term "moral" when referring to Israel's teachings. "In this respect it may be readily accepted that this instruction has little or no interest in acquiring theoretical knowledge, that it supplies, rather, pragmatic knowledge."[44] A moral instruction that is based on expediency is hardly worthy of the name. In addition to this, the Book of Proverbs contains very little admonition compared to the descriptive material which comprises the lion's share of the book. Most of the exhortation is found in 22:17—23:11, a section which parallels the Egyptian *Instruction of Amenemope.*

Examination of the content of the sayings in Proverbs has led von Rad to conclude that, while a "relatively well-placed middle class" is in the foreground, it would be incorrect to say that the book contains a class ethic. True, the life described is settled and secure. There appears to be no interest in altering the social structure. This suggests that the sayings originated with people who benefited from and were not exploited by these structures. However, because von Rad believes that the search for order was at the heart of the wisdom movement, he also believes that societal stability was the goal of all classes within the nation. Furthermore, he claims that orders or principles which promised this stability were valid for all. No one denies that the upper class had the upper hand. The question is whether or not Proverbs is the voice of the upper class.

Wisdom in Israel illustrates that the Book of Proverbs is a compilation of a multiplicity of individual sayings. It spans the intellectual activity of about eight centuries and incorporates the reflections of people from different social classes. It counsels and admonishes but chiefly it provides examples of various types of behavior and their consequences. Although adherence to Yahweh is seldom explicitly recommended, conformity to the orders within creation appears to be consistent with compliance with the will of

God. The book well deserves its reputation of being an anthology of the experiential wisdom of ancient Israel.

Whybray's goal in writing *The Intellectual Tradition of the Old Testament* was to propose and defend his theory that there was in ancient Israel *no* esoteric class of sages either at the court or in the schools. His treatment of the biblical material, notably the Book of Proverbs, is for the purpose of advancing this position. He neither surveys the content of nor examines the forms within the book. One must search behind his statements for traces of his understanding of the proverbs themselves.

He begins by mentioning the superscriptions of the seven sections of the book: 1:1 and 10:1 are attributed to Solomon; 25:1 to court scribes editing earlier Solomonic material; 30:1 and 31:1 to non-Israelite writers; 22:17 and 24:23 to unnamed men of superior intelligence or skill. Admitting the possibility that Solomonic authorship is a court tradition, he proceeds to enumerate other Solomonic traditions preserved in 1 Kings that are clearly Deuteronomic and in some cases of priestly origin while 2 Chronicles concentrates on interests of the priests of Jerusalem. Popular legendary material can be seen in the narratives of the two harlots and the queen of Sheba as well as in the Song of Solomon. It is certainly possible, claims Whybray, that the theory about Solomon's proficiency in wisdom and his authorship of proverbs could have arisen as popular tradition as well. The superscriptions of 1:1 and 10:1 merely suggest "no more than the expression of the popular belief that proverb-writing in Israel goes back to Solomon."[45] The reference in 25:1 indicates that the scribes of Hezekiah's court worked on earlier proverbial material that may or may not have been of court origin.

Although Whybray's study does not center on the content nor on the form of the various proverbs, he does not totally ignore them. He has already done this examination in an earlier work,[46] and here he merely summarizes his findings. He believes that chapters 1—9 of Proverbs are modeled after Egyptian Instructions which served as textbooks in the schools, but here the modeling ends. The circumstances under which they were composed differed—the court in Egypt versus general society in Israel—as did the circle of composers—professional Egyptian sages versus especially talented Israelite laypersons. While insisting upon a non-professional milieu as the cradle of the intellectual tradition, he concedes that the poetic statements which comprise the major portion of the book are not simply popular proverbs. They are carefully refined forms of parallel construction which could only have been developed within circles skilled in literary creativity. The admonition, a form which appears quite frequently in the Egyptian Instructions, does not enjoy the same prominence in Israel's literature. Its origin is a topic of considerable debate among scholars. Whybray holds that at least the first nine chapters of Proverbs have been directly influenced by older Near Eastern literatures. He does not believe, however, that this means that it was only within the court that such influence was felt. Non-courtly but intellectually sophisticated circles could very well have been affected by foreign writings.

Structure of the Book

Three articles found within *Studies in Ancient Israelite Wisdom* are relevant to the discussion on the Book of Proverbs. The first, and the most recent, is a study of the unity of the book by Patrick Skehan entitled "A Single Editor for the Whole Book of Proverbs."[47] In it Skehan attempts to prove that the author of chapters 1—9 is also the editor of essentially the entire book. Utilizing literary analysis, he showed in an earlier article[48] that this author carefully constructed an artificial framework for the first section of the book. Taking his findings one step further, Skehan claims that a similar method of composition can be detected throughout the rest of the book. This, along with the presence and development, in other parts of the book, of the first nine chapters, leads him to conclude to single editorship.

Rather than divide Proverbs into the customary eight, nine or ten sections, Skehan proposes four large blocks of text (1—9; 10:1—22:16; 22:17—24:34; 25—29; omitting 30—31), and applies the same type of literary analysis to the last three blocks as he did to the first one. He explains his approach in the following manner: "The discovery of a deliberate pattern of 7 x 22 lines for chapters 2 and 7 is the one quite new element which now prompts re-examination of our data regarding the rest of the book."[49] A comparable pattern is found in 10:1—22:16 where the entire collection consists of 375 single-line proverbs. This section is designated "Proverbs of Solomon," a title having the numerical value of 375. The thirty sayings in Proverbs 22:17—24:34 are said to be modeled after the thirty sections of the Egyptian *Instruction of Amenemope,* and the last unit, which is ascribed to "the men of Hezekiah," is a little more than 130 lines, the same numerical value for the Hebrew name Hezekiah. Each of the four major sections has internal numerical value, a structure either devised by one editor and imitated by subsequent editors or conceived by the final editor. Skehan contends that the latter is the case. He does this rather vividly with a chart showing the number of lines in each major section of the book as well as the numerical value of the titles of the superscription in 1:1. Admitting the possibility of several glosses in the text, Skehan arrives at a total number of 932 lines. Proverbs 1:1 identifies the collection as "The Proverbs of Solomon, son of David, king of Israel." The numerical value of the Hebrew words is as follows: Solomon is 375; David is 14; Israel is 541; the total is 930. From this Skehan concludes that the same person is responsible for the first nine chapters of the book with its significant superscription and for the artificial numerical structure of the rest of the book.

Anthropocentric Anthropology

The proverb is judged by Walter Zimmerli as "the normative form of the wisdom teaching, whose purest examplar is found in the Solomonic book of aphorisms."[50] He claims that this form expresses a total disposition toward life. His article "Concerning the Structure of Old Testament Wisdom" is an attempt to discover this disposition by carefully examining the form as well as the content of the proverb. Since the primary focus of the proverbs is appropriate human conduct, the underlying question has to do with the manner of living in the world. While the tenor of Qoheleth suggests that this author has withdrawn from the question in pessimistic resignation, the attitude in Proverbs is quite different. The optimistic conviction of knowing the answer permeates the positive statements of the book. Although Zimmerli treats both Qoheleth and Proverbs, only the latter will be considered here.

If the underlying question has to do with the manner of living in the world, then the perspective is genuinely anthropological. However, is it thereby also anthropocentric? Is its concern exclusively with the human agent? Is it the human agent as a member of the covenant community? If the latter be the case, the question changes from "How do I live in the world?" to "How do I, as a member of the covenant community, live in the world?" This anthropological perspective is plainly theocentric. All agree that the wisdom literature lacks reference to convenantal membership and responsibility, and that the implicit recognition of a cosmic order binding men and women is of only secondary importance. Nonetheless, any claim of a radical anthropocentric perspective is impossible. Zimmerli articulates the problem in this way: "Does the 'central question' of wisdom grow out of knowledge and recognition of a fixed, binding obligation ... or is the contention right that it is a question which originates with the individual person, ultimately being orientated around him alone?"[51] He attempts an answer to this problem by examining the inner structure of the wisdom command: "To what does it appeal when it attributes obedience to men?"[52]

A command demands obedience; counsel evokes deliberation and free choice. A command does not allow options; counsel is debatable. Most of the wisdom sayings are counsels and allow for various responses. Of themselves they contribute little to Zimmerli's investigation. It is to the direct admonitions and their organization and development that one must look to find an answer to his question.

It seems that it is relatively easy to transpose an admonition into an ordinary saying and vice versa. "Love not sleep, lest you come to poverty" (20:13) reads "The one who loves sleep will come to poverty." Experience demonstrates the truth of the saying from which a rule of conduct can be inferred. In this example, what authority lies behind the admonition? Is it a theological obligation? Is it cosmic order? Neither. The legitimation is experiential. Zimmerli concludes that "wisdom admonition lacks authoritative character. Its legitimation does not come about through any appeal to some authority."[53] When wisdom does assume the guise of personality, as in Proverbs 1—9, failure to follow its exhortation is not met with unexpected punishment. Rather, the fool must endure the consequences inherent in the chosen mode of conduct, consequences which could actually have been foreseen. Wisdom does not punish; it observes the preordained results of folly. The authority behind a wisdom admonition is human experience.

Turning to those proverbs which do contain theological elements, Zimmerli discovers that they speak of Yahweh conforming to human expectations, rewarding and punishing in accord with human behavior. God's involvement in the lives of women and men is measured in terms of the satisfaction, wealth and security it can bring to them. Even in these proverbs, utility is the standard for evaluation. Such an attitude is scarcely theocentric.

Utility is a relative standard. The "better than" proverbs are examples of this. This form affirms that some things are good but other things are better, and circumstances significantly alter the appropriateness of certain behavior. Good cannot be relativized where there is an authoritative standard, but here utility is the pragmatic standard of wisdom. Life is not examined according to its duties but rather according to its possibilities. The focus is not on any fixed limits but on incalculable prospects. The perspective here is definitely anthropocentric.

The one constant threat to this life of limitless possibilities is the specter of premature death. Proverbs does not deny it but pays far less attention to it than does Qoheleth. The reality of death forces him to modify the question to: "How do I keep myself from misfortune, especially premature death?" He acknowledges that he is not safe from such a death, for human destiny is in divine hands. He recognizes this though he rebels against it. His rebellion, which takes the form of skepticism and resignation, reveals that his anthropological perspective is basically anthropocentric, not theocentric. Human, not divine determination is his point of departure. As stated at the beginning of this discussion of Zimmerli's article, Qoheleth's withdrawal in pessimistic resignation was the only way he could deal with the conflict. This conflict is absent in the Book of Proverbs where divine determination and human freedom seem to intermingle harmoniously. This explains the optimistic attitude that is the hallmark of normative wisdom in ancient Israel.

Theocentric Anthropology

Twenty-eight years after Zimmerli's article appeared, Berend Gemser published "The Spiritual Structure of Biblical Aphoristic Wisdom."[54] It was a critique of Zimmerli's major points and a brief summary of four studies that have appeared since his penetrating work.

J. Coert Rylaarsdam's book *Revelation in Jewish Wisdom Literature* appeared in 1946. In it he claims that in all periods of Israel's history there was a concurrence of two convictions: wisdom was to be sought empirically through human experience, and it was at the same time a gift of God. He also shows a correspondence between wisdom and Deuteronomic teaching. Both traditions believe in a moral order, a world-affirming viewpoint, and similar virtues. His perspective is theocentric.

An opposing view is advanced by von Rad in his *Theologie des Alten Testaments.*[55] He distinguishes between older wisdom found in Proverbs 10ff, theological wisdom in 1—9, and a skeptical wisdom as found in Qoheleth. Wisdom grows out of life experiences and is based on a pre-supposed hidden order. The very literary forms give evidence of this order especially in the case of the numerical proverbs. This wisdom was cultivated at the court and subsequent schools. If early wisdom was anthropocentric, it was soon transformed into a theocentric perspective.

Two works appeared in 1958. One, "Die Proverbien und die Spruche von Jesus Sirach" by E.G. Bauckmann,[56] accepted all of the major points of Zimmerli and analyzed Ben Sira in light of them. From his anthropocentric point of view, Ben Sira has not taken over the letter and spirit of the Torah but has impressed the Torah with the stamp of wisdom. Torah thereby loses its authoritative character and becomes wisdom teaching, while wisdom becomes a form of theologizing.

The second work to appear that year was Hartmut Gese's *Lehre und Wiklichkeit.*[57] He stresses the similarities between the wisdom literature of Israel and the teachings of Egyptian sages. He opposes the notion that the teaching is eudaemonistic; its aim is to achieve harmony with world order. He claims that God dispenses good and evil independent of human expectations. This is clearly a theocentric view.

The second part of the article is Gemser's own critique of some of the points put forward in Zimmerli's study. He disagrees with Zimmerli's claim that the wisdom saying is not authoritative, quoting several instances in the biblical text where counsel of the wise is accorded the same force as the word of the prophet. He accuses Zimmerli of predicating Western thinking to the ancient Near Eastern mind, and he insists that counsel was not given without obligation.

If authority does lie behind the wisdom statement, whence is it derived? According to Zimmerli, authority flows from personality. Gemser calls this assertion another example of a limited Western way of thinking. Throughout the ancient Near East the concept of divine order was of fundamental importance. Parallel with it was the belief that wisdom was a prerogative of the deity and could only be bestowed by the gods. The following line of reasoning ensued: cosmic order is an expression of divine power and wisdom. Compliance with sapiential admonitions brings one into harmony with this cosmic order. The authority that lies behind these admonitions is divine.

One is led to ask: Is there any difference between the torah of the priest, the word of the prophet and the counsel of the wise? Gemser answers this question by citing Rylaarsdam who distinguishes between the vertical revelation of the prophet and priest and the horizontal revelation of the sage. All three groups of spiritual leaders call upon divine directives as motivation for conformity, even though they call upon them in different ways. The search for wisdom was but another way in one's journey to God.

Textbook for the Court?

It should be obvious by now that the identity of the milieu that gave birth to the didactic traditions of Israel is a topic of considerable debate. W. Lee Humphreys addressed this problem in an article published in *Israelite Wisdom* entitled "The Motif of the Wise Courtier in the Book of Proverbs."[58] He questions whether royal schools really did exist in Israel and suggests that the perceived need for such an institution and the known existence of convenient models in neighboring nations have led some to posit their existence in Israel as well. He belongs to those scholars who do not limit the use of the word "sage" to a professional group. He believes that the only reliable way of knowing whether or not any part of Proverbs was intended as an instruction for future courtiers is to do a careful study of the biblical material itself. This he attempts to do in the essay under discussion. His study is in two parts: an examination of Egyptian material destined for use in court schools; a careful scrutiny of Proverbs 10—29 with an eye to themes identical with or similar to those found in the Egyptian Instructions.

Humphreys limits his investigation to the Instruction of Ptah-hotep, Kagemni, Ani, and Amenemope. The works represent various levels of Egyptian government and different historical periods. In spite of these differences similarities in desired characteristics do surface. The courtier is to be humble and self-effacing in the presence of superiors but open and attentive to clients as well. He is to enjoy a family life beyond reproach and is to possess an unsullied reputation among his associates. He should not be given to excessive speech, but should not falter when his words are indispensable. These Instructions have been severely and inaptly criticized as selfishly pragmatic and purely secular. One must remember that Egypt's pharaoh was looked upon as divine. Service to the king was service to the god. The courtier was in compliance with cosmic order when he was attentive to royal desires and decrees. Ma'at governed the court as it did the heavens.

Turning to Proverbs 10—29, Humphreys divides the material into five sections: 10:1—15:33; 16:1—22:16; 22:17—24:34; 25:1—27:27; 28:1—29:27. He bases this division on formal structure, headings and content, examining each division in order. He first treats royal sayings that speak directly to the situation of the courtier and then addresses themes that correspond to a motif found within Egyptian Instructions.

The first collection (10—15) contains only two references to the king. Teaching directed exclusively to a court official plays only a minor role in this collection.

The orientation is quite different in the second unit (16:1—22:16). Great emphasis is placed on correct speech and self-mastery. Chapters 16 and 21—22 contain groups of king-sayings, instructions for winning royal favor. There is also the image of the throne supported by righteousness. Within the Egyptian tradition, Ma'at was the foundation of natural, special and political order. The closest Hebrew equivalent to the concept of Ma'at is Righteousness. With the establishment of the monarchy, the throne assumed this same characteristic because it was confirmed by Yahweh the God of Righteousness. The establishment and safeguarding of justice in the land was one of the chief responsibilities of the king. These chapters of Proverbs contain both royal and divine sayings, a distinction necessary in the theology of Israel but irrelevant for Egyptian thought.

The influence of the *Instructions of Amenemope* upon the third collection (22:17—24:34) has long been recognized. The structure is patterned after the thirty chapters of the Egyptian work, and the perspective of the courtier is obvious in several proverbs. While this theme was prominent in the Egyptian Instruction and was probably carried into Proverbs from this source, it is not, according to Humphreys, the controlling motif of the collection.

One must move on to the fourth collection (25—29) for material directed toward the training of court officials. In the fifth collection (28—29) the perspective is quite different. Here the addressee is the king. Some look upon this shift as evidence of Israelite adaptation, for the admonitions directed to the king are similar to Deuteronomic exhortation. To accept this position uncritically is to overlook the Egyptian *Instruction of Meri-ka-re,* a king's advice to his son.

What conclusions can be drawn from this examination? Humphreys claims that the motif of the wise courtier plays a minor role in the collections studied. In only two collections (16:1—22:16 and 25:2–7) does the motif enjoy a controlling position. Wherever else it appears, it is addressed to a general audience. Within Egyptian society, service at the court was esteemed as the highest ideal of a good and pious life, because loyalty to the king was loyalty to the god. The situation was quite different in Israel principally because of the distinction between the divine and the royal spheres. In Egypt, service at the divine royal court had a theological dimension to it. Such was not the situation in Israel. Both the demythologization of royal ideology and the importance of circles other than the court as centers of education influenced the developmental history of Proverbs. Humphrey suggests the possibility of commercial and mercantile circles as formative influences. Like the court, they were exposed to foreign influences and would be attentive to middle or upper class concerns. In any case, this study contends that Proverbs is not the manual for the training of future officials.

4
Job

The Book of Job has long been considered a classic of world literature. The reason for this has been explained in several ways. The struggle of the innocent sufferer, a universal phenomenon, consistently occupies the time and energy of those committed to justice. In fact, every life can witness to suffering that is either unwarranted or unexplained. Each woman and man must grapple with this inevitable reality and must acknowledge that adversity cannot be avoided and, unfortunately, often remains inexplicable. In such a dilemma, many turn to the Book of Job wherein they can find and identify with a righteous person who is beset with misfortune and anxiety.

The very literary form of the book invites universal acclaim. It is a composite of various types of literature and styles of writing. The final product allows for several theological interpretations, thereby expanding the applicability of the message to a broad audience. This flexibility accounts for the book's appeal to people of every class and ideology of both ancient and modern times.

A brief look at the structure of the work will reveal several units which individually possess unique artistic quality and together create a literary composition that has seldom been rivaled. The book can be divided into two major pieces: a prose prologue (1:1—2:13) and epilogue (42:7—17) which were probably drawn from an ancient folktale and here provide a framework for the major section, and a poetic dialogue (3:1—42:6) composed of several exchanges between

Job and his visitors followed by speeches from Yahweh. The manner in which one understands the relationships among the sections will influence the way one interprets the entire book.

One of the most disputed questions in Joban studies is the meaning of the Yahweh speeches. Does God ignore Job's pleas and demands and bring him to his knees, humbling him for his brazenness? If this is the case, were Job's visitors correct in chastising him for arrogance? Or, on the other hand, does Yahweh reveal the divine wisdom and power only to instill in this broken human being a trust in God that not even incomprehensible tragedy can shake? With what is the author of the book really struggling? Innocent suffering? Disinterested piety? Trust in the deity? The ineffability of God? Human limitations? A challenge to divine justice? The credibility of God? The inadequacy of any theory of retribution, or of world order for that matter? The drama of the Book of Job continues to hold the minds and hearts of women and men, partially because no one of these solutions alone adequately answers all of the questions raised by the book, and partially because new studies continue to throw light on different aspects of the work.

Confidence in a World of Order

Within the chapter of *Wisdom in Israel* entitled "Trust and Attack" von Rad treats both Job and Ecclesiastes. Since the two works deal with related questions it seems appropriate to summarize the general world view underlying both and to highlight the relationship between that world view and the actual struggles described. Von Rad does this by drawing some implications of the notion of order. He claims that ancient Israel did not approach knowledge in an objective and detached manner. Rather, those who sought after knowledge of the orders within the universe wholeheartedly committed themselves to these orders once they were discerned. These orders could be trusted; indeed, they had to be trusted, for therein lay the only security one could know. Observation of the conformity to these orders constituted the path to a successful life.

Experience showed this to be true and thus the orders were to be trusted. This explains the optimism and conviction with which the sages expressed themselves. They entertained no doubt about the reliability of the orders of the universe nor about the outcome of certain actions. The unqualified nature of proverbial expression illustrates this. The sages credited God with the establishment and maintenance of these orders and, therefore, they made no distinction between trust in the order and trust in God. In fact, it was precisely within the parameters of this order that the blessings of life were accorded to those who proved to be faithful to Yahweh. This was not merely the teaching of those who currently enjoyed pedagogical influence. It was at the very heart of a long teaching tradition, and examples of the validity of this tradition could be found throughout Israel's history. One must not accuse Israel of understanding this order as a rigid system of laws. Rather, it was seen as the manner in which God acted toward the world. To acquire this knowledge was to know something about God, and vice versa. The statement about the fear of the Lord being the beginning of wisdom could be reversed. As fear of the Lord led to wisdom, so wisdom led to fear of the Lord.

If the world view to which one subscribes is based on some form of order or regularity, how is one to understand and deal with the ambiguity with which life is fraught? How does one explain suffering? Israel believed in a Creator-God and in the oneness of creation. There was no room in such a belief system for a competing power of evil and destruction. When experiences of life were too ambiguous or contradictory, the entire system of order was threatened along with religious trust in the God responsible for that system. Rather than challenge the entire system Israel advanced several tentative solutions for the dilemma. The suffering might be some kind of purification for past failures still unrequited. Perhaps it was a test which offered the sufferer an opportunity to prove the quality of trust in God that had been previously professed. Maybe it was a form of discipline intended to prepare the devotee for future challenge and deeper commitment. With the exception of the first explanation— that of delayed punishment—these solutions create more problems than they solve. None of them hints at why a wise God should so act toward limited human beings. The drama of Job is played out on stage of order and trust. The incomprehensibility of the dilemma confounds any rigid system of order and threatens any unquestioning trust in God.

Confidence in a Mysterious God

Von Rad's interpretation of Job is based on his analysis of only the poetic section. He does not deal directly with the prologue and epilogue. He feels that the theological differences between the dialogue and the prose "folk narrative" are too great to provide a satisfactory link. Therefore, he confines his investigation to the dialogue and the struggles that are present there.

Job is a man who is steeped in his religious tradition and the thought-forms of his day which articulate that tradition. Von Rad suggests that Job may even be more immersed in them than are his self-appointed counselors. This would account for much of the pain and frustration that he experiences. Like them he operates from a clearly ordered world view which perceives suffering as the consequence of human behavior. Like them he is convinced that God is responsible for his affliction. Unlike them he will not, indeed he cannot, admit that he is guilty of misbehavior and deserving of punishment. His visitors argue from the principle of order, in this case from the theory of retribution. Job argues from the reality of experience, his experience. Being righteous he had a proper relationship with God and enjoyed the fruits of this relationship. He no longer enjoys these fruits but has done nothing to alter the relationship. He knows this; his companions do not, and they will not believe him when he makes his claim.

Job also rejects the suggestion that he is suffering for the sins of others. He demands that he be judged on his own merits. Von Rad explains this attitude as the result of movement toward a kind of personalism that began to develop at the end of the monarchy. The mystery associated with individual life began to present problems for the tightly organized system of established Yahwism. The religion of the later period "revealed itself less and less as a firm complex of connected ideas."[59]

What precisely does Job claim? Von Rad sees this claim as threefold: he protects his righteousness in the face of what appears to be overwhelming evidence to the contrary; he demands an explanation from God, the one responsible for his plight; he admits the hopelessness of any prospect of redress. At this point one cannot avoid the question of divine justice.

His own unique experience leads Job into a new vision of divine activity vis-à-vis human suffering. Job's God is not a punitive God, for this cannot be punishment. Rather, Job depicts God as a ravenous beast that delights in tearing the helpless human apart. This is his present experience, so unlike that of the provident God of the past. This is torment, not testing or discipline. Job's demand for justice springs from the wisdom concern for order, but the image of God with which he struggles is the Savior God of ancient Israel. Will God act as Savior for Job? "It is not suffering, as has so often been said, which has become so utterly problematic, but God."[60] It is no longer a question of trusting the God of order. The challenge is rather: Can Job trust a God who is totally free and whose activities are in conflict with recognized order?

The divine response explicitly accuses Job of only one thing. He, a mere human, has interfered in God's affairs. Job is never dismissed by God. He is instructed. All of the questioning about the universe serves one purpose. It brings to center stage both the majesty and the mystery of the universe. All of creation bears witness to God. The resolution of Job's dilemma comes when he withdraws his challenge and thereby acknowledges "that his destiny, too, is well protected by this mysterious God."[61]

A Unique Literary Form

While von Rad's investigation is concerned with theological matters, Whybray is interested in certain literary characteristics of the book. In *The Intellectual Tradition in the Old Testament* his treatment of the Joban material is in the form of comparison with Proverbs. Acknowledging that the speeches of Job and his companions contain abundant examples of individual proverbial statements similar to those found in Proverbs, Whybray insists that they serve different purposes in each book. Proverbs is very didactic, offering instruction in every section. The book does not contain prolonged discussion of problems as does Job. However, Job does not offer any clear solution for the problems under discussion. This is probably due to the fact that the author is investigating an issue for which there seems to be no clear answer. Job is not didactic; it is reflective.

Another point that occupies Whybray's attention is the literary form of the book. The biblical author has utilized several different forms within the composition itself: lawsuit, individual lament, in addition to the prose narrative framework. There is significant disagreement as regards the basic form of the total work. Several commentators do not even consider it an example of wisdom literature. Some classify it as an individual lament. Others see the dialogue as a form of disputation, a technique popular within the "wisdom schools." Since the major thesis of Whybray's book is the refutation of an organized wisdom movement, established wisdom schools, and a professional class of sages in ancient Israel, he would not be convinced by these arguments. In fact, he feels that the book itself strengthens his argument. Neither Job nor any of his visitors is portrayed as a professional sage. He appears to be a once wealthy land owner. They act toward him as he had previously acted toward others. They appear to be his peers and, therefore, educated farmers. Toward the end of the dialogue a fourth man, Elihu, insists that he excels his elders in speaking to Job's problem. His claim that neither seniority nor length of experience guarantees competence is a far cry from any "wisdom school's" claim to superiority.

In many ways the Book of Job is, according to Whybray, so unique and different from traditional wisdom teaching that it is difficult to see the author as a member of a tradition-bound professional literary class. Whybray describes the work as individual and unique but he does not throw light on the question as to why this is the case. He credits the author with an unusual vocabulary and a style found nowhere else in the Hebrew tradition, but he seems satisfied merely to make that statement and then go on to the next point.

The Problem with Retribution

Although Matitiahu Tsevat's article "The Meaning of the Book of Job" first appeared in 1966, the quality of insight and the skillfulness with which the author presents his argument have earned it a place in Crenshaw's anthology *Studies in Ancient Israelite Wisdom.* Tsevat contends that the book poses several questions. At the outset, the Satan challenges Job's integrity. Is there disinterested piety? God accepts the challenge and thereby sets the meaning of piety for the rest of the book. It can only be attached to that action which is performed without expectation of material reward. Tsevat further states that the problem of the book is the suffering of the innocent. He disagrees with those who assert that the book offers no answer to this problem, since he claims that this answer is found in the final chapters of the poetic section. The theophany seems to have assuaged Job's torments. Futhermore, in the epilogue Yahweh speaks as if the dilemma has been resolved. It is within the theophany, therefore, that the answer is to be found.

To those who claim that the theophany itself and not its content is the answer, Tsevat replies: "The event of a revelation, distinct from its specific, articulate content, is personal, untransmissible, and unrepeatable."[62] If the theophany alone were the answer, each sufferer would have to have a personal revelation. This cannot be the case. Instead, a close examination of the content of the divine speeches will uncover the solution. Tsevat does just that.

In chapters 38–42, Yahweh questions Job as to his whereabouts at the time of creation, his comprehension of its inner workings and its full expanse, his knowledge of and control over wild animals. After being interrogated in this way, Job is asked whether he will persist in his demands. Has the revelation of God had any effect on him? Both of Job's responses (40:4–5; 42:2–6) clearly show that it has. What exactly has affected him and in what way? Obviously the revelation itself has. It shows that Job has not been rejected by God; his demand to meet God has been answered. This in itself is a kind of vindication. Nor did he have to sacrifice anything for this encounter. He had pleaded for some kind of understanding of the world and he was awarded it, though not as he had expected.

Before he offers his own interpretation of the theophany, Tsevat reviews and critiques four of the more popular explanations. The first is what he calls "education through overwhelming." Job is overwhelmed by the magnificence of the universe and is brought to submission. Tsevat counters this view by pointing out that Job never doubted divine power and wisdom. He asserted that this very power and wisdom had been turned against him. The second solution proposed has to do with divine justice. It is not like human justice, retributory and egalitarian. The revelation shows that God gives what is appropriate to each. Tsevat disclaims this, for at the heart of

Job's frustration is the undue severity of his plight. A third view suggests that the panoramic beauty of the universe acts as a balm for this man whose whole being is an open wound. Tsevat wonders how beauty can be expected to answer the demands of justice. The fourth interpretation attacks the question of the problem. Rather than ask "*Why* do the innocent suffer?" one should ask "*How* should the innocent suffer?" Such a position alters the entire thrust of the book. The answer would not be found in the revelation but in Job's response to it. Tsevat rejects this outright and insists that the question to be answered is *why,* not *how.*

His own approach to the interpretation is threefold: an evaluation of the total conceptual content; an analysis of passages from the divine address; a critique of the answer using external evidence. He begins by pointing out the basic world view shared by Job and his visitors. They believed that the world is founded on justice, *quid pro quo,* measure for measure. Job would never demand an explanation for his predicament were this not the case, nor would his counselors insist on some hidden guilt. Tsevat maintains that it is this world view that must be altered: ". . . only the awareness that the world of ideas, unlike the world of matter, is not governed by the category of cause and effect, i.e., only the elimination of the principle of retribution, can solve the problem of the book."[63]

Three passages from the Yahweh speeches indicate that the revelation intends to do just that. Job 38:12f, and 38:15 suggest that the natural world is not concerned with retribution. The sun rises on the sinner as well as on the righteous. Job contends that retribution is at least potentially operative in the world. If he can effect it even God will applaud him (40:8–14). The third passage is described as "least conspicuous but the most interesting." Rain was considered the vehicle of reward or punishment. The righteous were blessed with it while the wicked were denied it. Job 38:25–27 states that it falls on wasteland where it benefits no one and nothing. The moral purpose assigned to water does not really exist. Laws of the natural order and those of the moral order are not the same.

The verification of this interpretation is found in the prologue. The reader knows from the very first chapter of the book that Job's predicament is not the consequence of his behavior. The theory of retribution does not provide the answer to Job's dilemma.

The dating of this book can throw light on the discussion. Most scholars situate Job somewhere between the sixth and the fourth centuries B.C.E. (Before the Common Era). This was a time when the earlier doctrine of collective retribution worked out in future generations had lost its influence and a later doctrine of individual retribution in an afterlife had not yet gained acceptance. Job reflects a radical denial of the theory but offers nothing in its place. Over the centuries many have wondered why the author has been so oblique in presenting the solution to the problem. Tsevat believes that because of its radical nature the new teaching could not be put forward more directly. If even today, in an apparently more liberal world, the religious rebel is often suspect and rejected, how much more likely this would be in the ancient world with its understandable fear of radical individuality.

Tsevat summarizes this investigation using an equilateral triangle. At one vertex is God, at another is Job, and at the third is retribution. The three points cannot co-exist. The counselors insist on God and retribution and thus reject Job. God has canceled retribution in favor of God and Job. Job all but gives up God in favor of himself and retribution. The key phrase is "all but." The theophany shows that Job, even in error, was closer to the truth than were his counselors. The resolution of the book shows that the one who speaks to Job from the whirlwind is neither just nor unjust but God.

Caricatures of Job

Israelite Wisdom contains an article by John Gammie entitled "Behemoth and Leviathan: On the Didactic and Theological Significance of Job 40:15—41:26." This is a highly specialized study of the two flamboyant creatures of the second divine speech. Although much has been written about these monsters, the identification of their nature and of the role they play in the book continues to occupy the interest of scholarship. Gammie provides yet another perspective on the topic.

Scholars are divided as to the nature of the beasts. The same biblical description has led some to classify them as mythical monsters and others to consider them natural animals. Gammie suggests that they are instead characterizations of Job. He contends that they do more than merely enhance the description of the mysterious creative wisdom and power of God. They speak directly to Job's suffering and protest.

The second divine discourse can easily be divided into three parts: an introduction (40:6–14), the behemoth pericope (40:15–24), and the Leviathan pericope (40:25—41:26). Gammie does a meticulous examination of each. He suggests that because Job has attempted to put God in the wrong (v 8) he, Job, should be included with the wicked (v 12). The author of Job then proceeds to describe the "wicked" Behemoth and Leviathan as types of human endeavor, or of Job himself.

Juvel as Behemoth

The initial literary analysis of the Behemoth pericope does not preclude a mythical understanding of the beast. However, Gammie points to three features in 40:15 that suggest that this is an animal of the natural world. (1) The word "Behold" implies that the creature can be seen. (2) That the beast was made "as I made you" hints at the material character of both. (3) "He eats grass like cattle" and is thereby compared with other natural animals. There is another reference in v 23 that plays a significant part in this argument. When the river troubles the beast and the waters come up to its mouth, it does not flee in fear but remains serene. Here Behemoth is not seen as an opponent of God but as one who is confident even in the face of adversity.

Gammie draws five conclusions from his analysis: (1) The Almighty does not slay the beast but tempers its anger. (2) Job is correct in his claim that God has sought him out but is mistaken in appraising God's motive. (3) When oppressed, Behemoth does not flee but remains confident. (4) As Job was brought to darkness, so Behemoth is forced to dwell in the river's shades. (5) Both Job and Behemoth have retained regenerative powers. Gammie sees Behemoth as a didactic and consoling image which speaks directly to Job's suffering and loss.

The Leviathan pericope is treated in a comparable manner. Mythical features are admitted as are characteristics associated with the crocodile. There are, nonetheless, four facts which make the present interpretation difficult to dismiss: (1) Job likens himself to Leviathan (3:8). (2) Leviathan has no equal "on the dust" (41:33), a position that Job has taken throughout the book (2:8; 30:19; 42:6).

(3) Leviathan is further called "king of all majestic wild beasts" (41:34). (4) Job has been described with royal imagery (31:37); Gammie presents this as evidence that the author intended that Leviathan be seen, at least in part, as a figure of Job. This animal that thrashes in the water also gives off flashes of light. It illustrates that wisdom comes to light in the midst of struggle.

Thus Gammie portrays Behemoth and Leviathan as caricatures of Job. They struggle within their own habitat but respond, in the midst of conflict, with confidence and fidelity.

The Book of Job continues to be a challenge to the scholar as well as a comfort to the believer. The multiplicity of interpretations, diverse as they may be, only contributes to the attraction of the book. For while one may not understand or agree with one or another interpretive approach, the dilemma portrayed is known to all and the search for understanding is universal.

5
Qoheleth

from Luther
der Prediger

A second book included within the category of wisdom literature which challenges the traditional and predictable teaching of the
sages is Ecclesiastes or Qoheleth. The former title, Ecclesiastes,
comes from the Greek translation of the Hebrew word Qoheleth.
The latter word is derived from the root for "assembly" and refers to
the one who conducts the assembly or runs the school—hence the ?
designation "The Preacher." In addition to its somewhat unorthodox
teaching, the book is like Job in that it consists of basically one
external literary form. This form, namely the Royal Testament, is
seldom found within the sacred writings of ancient Israel but was
quite popular in ancient Egypt. Composed of several didactic poems
and proverbial statements, the composition is expressed in the first
person and purports to be a testimony of the sage's personal experience of life. In the very first chapter of Qoheleth (the name that will
be used throughout this study) the speaker is identified as "son of
David, king of Israel" (1:1, 12). This designation may have enabled
the author to ascribe Solomonic authority to an otherwise questionable speculative work. Since Solomon was considered patron of the
wisdom movement and the Royal Testament was a form associated
with monarchy, the book has never been totally rejected by the
believing community in spite of its radical nature.

The Book of Qoheleth is not merely a collection of personal
musings and ramblings. There are several major themes that act as
unifying agents. They are: "vanity," "striving after wind," "toil,"

and "portion." After examining the events and happenings of life, Qoheleth analyzes them against the sobering background of these themes. He is less concerned with individual actions or events than he is with the totality of life itself.

God and the Meaning of Life

As mentioned earlier, von Rad treats both Job and Qoheleth in *Wisdom in Israel* in the chapter entitled "Trust and Attack." He claims that three major insights emerge around which all of Qoheleth's thought circles. An explanation of these points comprises von Rad's study of the book.

The first point can be very clearly stated: Life is vanity! Throughout the book Qoheleth makes many statements that would lead one to draw this conclusion. Experience bears out the validity of these statements. There seems to be little if any relationship between the toil one must undertake and the fruits that accrue from it. The structure of society does not offer a reassuring picture. It seems that injustice rules in the place of justice. Integrity and order appear to be of no account. The wicked often prosper while the righteous are downtrodden, and in the end all must face the same fate—death. What may be worst of all is the fact that human beings have no control over the future. They are at its mercy. It is not surprising that one like Qoheleth would claim that life is vanity. Not even the wisdom that is associated with age seems capable of altering any of this apparent inequity. Contemporary women and men are in agreement with Qoheleth when they say: Life is meaningless!

The second point of von Rad's analysis heightens the drama. Qoheleth does not interpret this state of affairs as evidence of haphazard fate. He acknowledges that there is some power that determines each event and he usually refers to this phenomenon as "time." Everything has its time. Qoheleth believes in a certain determinism, and behind this determinism is God. Humans cannot alter this; they must submit to it.

Having judged life as vain and God as responsible for the orders of reality, Qoheleth, according to von Rad, makes what may well be his most radical claim. Humans are unable to discern these orders and are thereby unable to master life. The real burden of human life is not adversity. It is, rather, the insurmountable barrier which prevents the acquisition of necessary understanding. If there is within each person a thirst for knowledge, what value has life if that thirst cannot be quenched? The only course to take is to hold oneself open for whatever good things God will grant and then enjoy them whenever they come. Von Rad insists on the clear distinction between the advice to enjoy whatever can enhance life and the temptation to settle for hedonistic living in the face of despair. Qoheleth has been inappropriately accused of the latter when the former is closer to the truth.

Both Job and Qoheleth insist that there is no satisfactory explanation for some things in life. Life is vanity! They are also in agreement as to the existence of certain orders in the universe with God responsible for them. They part company at the third point. Job insists that he should be able to discern the manner of divine activity in the world, while Qoheleth claims that this is impossible. He goes one step further. Besides insisting that such discernment is beyond human perception and comprehension, he claims that men and women are incapable of adapting to this situation. It is not enough that the mastery of life is beyond human reach; the very yearning to achieve mastery has been quelled. The old wisdom teaching may have been too optimistic; Qoheleth appears to have lost all optimism. No sage would have presumed understanding of "the whole work of God." Still Qoheleth insists that "all is vanity."

What makes Qoheleth so different from older sages or, for that matter, even Job? Unlike those whose experience was in constant dialogue with faith, Qoheleth had lost trust in the orders of the universe. They failed to reveal to him any kind of reliable divine activity. According to ancient faith, the future was the domain of Yahweh alone. For Qoheleth, the hiddenness of this future was the greatest burden of a burdensome life. One could not look to the future to right wrongs. The only option left was the enjoyment of the present to the extent that it could be enjoyed. Qoheleth attempts to answer the questions of life, even the question of salvation, mainly on the basis of his experience of the world around him. This is what makes his answer so scandalous. He denies any possible dialogue with the world. It can tell him nothing with certainty. Von Rad holds that Qoheleth could only enter into dialogue with the world when it offered him some kind of fulfillment. If this is the case, Qoheleth was anything but a religious man and he deserves the indictment filed against him. He is a skeptic, a cynic, even a hedonist. While his own judgment may not be this harsh, von Rad does not present Qoheleth in a very favorable light.

The Intellectual Tradition in the Old Testament has little to add to this discussion of Qoheleth. Whybray disagrees with von Rad regarding the overall form of the book. He views it as an unorganized "mass of unrelated short pieces like the larger part of Proverbs."[64] He further holds that the characteristic vocabulary indicates that, while Qoheleth was familiar with the style of earlier proverbial literature, he probably composed many of his own proverbs. Whybray agrees with von Rad that Qoheleth is pessimistic and passionless and possesses a detached attitude quite unique in the Hebrew tradition. One must turn to *Studies in Ancient Israelite Wisdom* for a more positive analysis of the book.

Enjoyment Is in the Doing

The first of two articles that offer a favorable look at Qoheleth is "What Does It Profit a Man?: The Wisdom of Qoheleth" by James Williams. The author identifies two characteristic literary features of Qoheleth: its creative use of traditional wisdom, and its employment of rhetorical questions that call for negative answers. These features have earned Qoheleth the distinction of being classified as a wisdom teacher. Williams interprets the "confessional style" of the book as a sign of crisis within the wisdom tradition. He speaks of Qoheleth's pessimistic-skeptical attitude and attributes it to his recognition of the discrepancy between the human appetite for wisdom and the impossibility of its being satisfied. Qoheleth draws conclusions about life and the world from his personal and individual experience and not from the collected time-honored experience of the community. Having moved away from the traditional community understanding of reality, he is left with a sense of emptiness and meaninglessness.

Williams bases his understanding of Qoheleth on his study of three key words: "vanity" as contrasted with *olam,* "profit," and "portion." He asserts that for Qoheleth the primary question for human existence is the value of the individual within the total environment. Qoheleth insists that every human endeavor is vain, and the recognition of this alienates women and men from the world. This alienation appears to be "unhealable" because God has put *olam* in the human heart. Scholars translate this Hebrew word in several ways: love of the world, everlasting, or hidden wisdom. Whatever the translation, *olam* is that which lies at the core of existence and draws human beings toward God. Nothing can satisfy the human heart but *olam* and to run after anything else is vain. But *olam* is beyond human reach—consequently the frustration and the sense of alienation. Thus Williams argues that "*olam* is the opposite of vapor and is at the root of vain human striving."[65]

Williams further insists that Qoheleth is a religious man. If *olam* is the divine dimension of reality and Qoheleth acknowledges that everything is empty except *olam,* then his is a religious insight. Like the prophets, Qoheleth is an iconoclast, rejecting all easy answers, even religious answers. His search is grounded in concern for the ultimate reality.

Turning to the remaining key words, "profit" and "portion," Williams maintains that though they are interrelated the words are not identical. Qoheleth can see no "profit" in anything that perishes or that cannot be held as an advantage or surplus. This applies to toil, pleasure, even wisdom. The only thing that has any "profit" is life itself, even if it is a vapor. In the face of all this there is yet a "portion" offered to each human being. It is to have immediate enjoyment of whatever is found. One must not be preoccupied with consequences or rewards, but must rejoice in the very midst of what is being done. "Real life is finding one's portion in partaking of, and partaking in, the good things: what is pleasant or responsive to consciousness or human being. But, one cannot profit from them; one can only enjoy them."[65a]

While Williams agrees that Qoheleth is a skeptic, he will not call him a pessimist, nor will he label him a hedonist. He writes that Qoheleth speaks of a profit-portion and a joy-portion, and opts for the joy-portion. Profit-portion falls within the range of traditional wisdom teaching. Hedonism implies that pleasure is sought for its own sake. Qoheleth teaches that it is in the process of doing what life demands that joy will be found. Pleasure is not the goal; it is found in the doing.

To Williams, Qoheleth is a man whose words shatter fixation on all human accomplishment. Nothing that can be seen or heard or touched or smelled or tasted is the final reality, although the *olam* may be hidden within everything. He sees Qoheleth as a sage who has had a profound and authentic human experience but who does not yet have the adequate symbols and language to express it. But then this is the situation of most iconoclasts.

The Incomprehensibilty of God's Work

A second and more technical study found within this anthology is "The Riddle of the Sphinx: The Structure of the Book of Qoheleth" by Addison G. Wright. It is an analysis from a structural approach. Like the sphinx, Qoheleth presents the reader with more riddles than answers. However, there is growing consensus among scholars on several issues of the book. For one, there appears to be a move away from regarding Qoheleth as a hedonist, a pessimist or an agnostic. Commentators recognize that no one label expresses the complexity of the man or of his work.

Wright states his thesis at the beginning of the article. He believes that the book possesses a definite structure and that this structure is found in three successive patterns of verbal repetition. Recognition of this structure will reveal a straightforward presentation of the major theme of the book. Before unfolding his own position, Wright summarizes previous views regarding the structure of the book. Scholars have either denied the existence of any structure at all, or they have devised so many and such diverse plans that the lack of agreement is seen as evidence that there was no plan in the first place.

Wright identifies himself with a new school of literary criticism known as New Criticism or New Stylistics. It is a move away from the psychological, historical and biographical approaches to literature, placing the point of departure within the work itself and applying the principles of structural analysis. The New Critics attempt to be as objective as possible, concentrating on the form of the work and not primarily on the apparent progression of thought. They are concerned with repetitions of vocabulary and grammatical forms. They believe that such repetitions might provide a key to the thought of the author. They take notice of significant literary changes as well as obvious similarities. All of these considerations contribute to the discernment of the structural patterns within the work.

Before presenting his very detailed analysis of the units he has isolated, Wright provides an overview of his findings. He is in the mainstream of interpretation when he states that the book gets underway in 1:12. In addition to the introductory unit (1:1–11), he sets aside the closing poem (11:7—12:8) for later examination. He perceives three successive patterns embracing all of the material between 1:12 and 11:6. He claims that where one pattern ends the next begins. These patterns suggest that the book can be divided into two main parts, 1:12–6:9 and 6:10—11:6. The first he calls "Qoheleth's Investigation of Life" and the second he labels "Qoheleth's Conclusions." In the first part Qoheleth is concerned with the vanity or emptiness of various human endeavors, and in the second with humankind's inability to understand the work of God. The second part of the book can be further divided into two sections which parallel each other in structuring techniques. These three distinct divisions are all composed of units of thought which end with verbal patterns peculiar to each particular division.

The first section begins with 1:12–15, an introductory statement ending with "all is vanity and a chase of the wind" followed by a proverb. A parallel introduction is found in 1:16–18 which ends with "a chase after wind" and a proverb. Two paragraphs follow, each ending with "all was vanity and a chase after wind." Thus a pattern has been established which can be detected in five more places: 2:26, twice in 4:46, again in 4:16, and finally in 6:9 where it ends, never to be repeated. What does Qoheleth discover as he investigates life? "All is vanity and a chase after wind."

When this pattern ceases in 6:9, two new ideas are immediately introduced: one does not know what good to do, and one does not know what the future holds. The first idea is developed in 7:1—8:17, each unit of that section ending with the phrase "find out." The final unit (8:17) ends with a triple "cannot find out." The second idea is developed in 9:1—11:6 where each unit is marked by "do not know" or "no knowledge," and the final unit (11:5–6) ends with a triple "you do not know."

Wright is convinced that his findings should be the basis of any future exegesis of the book, and that the material that falls within the units he has delineated should be interpreted within that context. He does not claim that his interpretation is totally accurate, but he wishes to begin the interpretation in this fashion.

The last section of the article discusses the introductory poem as well as the concluding poem on old age. He believes that the phrase "vanity of vanities, all is vanity" found in 1:2 forms one boundary of an overall inclusion for the book. The other is found in 12:8. He further states that the question about gain that is asked in 1:3 provides the context for what follows in the rest of the poem. "There is no profit in toil because nothing is gained, neither progress, novelty, nor remembrance."[66]

The poem on old age, with which the book closes, reinforces Qohelth's advice on enjoyment. One is told to enjoy what can be enjoyed while it can be enjoyed, for darkness is coming when all this will cease.

Wright claims that Qoheleth speaks quite clearly about the major theme of the book, namely, the impossibility of understanding the work of God. The only advice that Qoheleth gives is to enjoy life and the fruit of one's labor while this is possible.

Qoheleth and Death

One of the major themes to which any discussion of Qoheleth eventually turns is death. This is the specific topic of an article appearing in the collection *Israelite Wisdom.* In "The Shadow of Death in Qoheleth," James Crenshaw uses a study of Job by Samuel Terrien as the point of departure for his investigation. Terrien had traced Job's attitude toward death through three stages: hatred of life leads to love of death; desire for death rather than risking unfaithfulness to God; fascination for death gives way to fear of death. Crenshaw discovered that, like Job, Qoheleth was ambiguous in his attitudes toward life and death. There are fundamental differences between the attitudes represented in the two characters. For Job death threatened the possibility of his vindication and thereby his trust in God. Qoheleth experiences no need for vindication and appears devoid of any trust in a divine being.

Crenshaw highlights three attitudes toward death expressed by Qoheleth. The first is found in the initial chapters of the book. After having conducted a series of experiments in an effort to find the value of human striving, Qoheleth concluded, "So I hated life because the work that is done under the sun is burdensome to me; for everything is empty and a chasing after wind" (2:17). This attitude flies in the face of the traditional priestly, prophetic, or sapiential thought of ancient Israel. There death symbolizes the evil all sought to avoid. It was the punishment for infidelity, not something to be desired. In early Yahwistic traditions an incomprehensible or untimely death was countenanced only because of the communitarian notion of corporate personality. In this mode of thinking, the blessings that had been withheld from the righteous would accrue to their descendants. Even a cursory reading of Qoheleth makes clear his total rejection of any of this thought. According to him, death is favored over life and there is no guarantee that the offspring of the righteous are any more favored than the posterity of the wicked. Crenshaw would have the reader remember that Qoheleth's disenchantment with life arose from his conviction that it was meant to be embraced wholeheartedly. This is a man who cherished the delights of living. He was far from being innately pessimistic. Forced to admit that wholehearted living was often impossible, he appears to have lost confidence in life itself. Devoid of justice, life is hollow and death is preferred.

Secondly, Qoheleth takes a positive view of death as a rest from adversity. He has been unjustly accused by some commentators of being insensitive to social injustice. The sufferings endured by the oppressed are the very reason he looks to death for deliverance. But until it comes, life is to be lived as fully as possible. Women and men must squeeze out every drop of enjoyment that it offers, not for the sake of some future gain, but for the sake of the moment. Once again Qoheleth's apparent cynicism stems from his appreciation of a satisfying existence.

Qoheleth's third view of death is a supposedly positive view toward life. He claims that the living have some hope. Crenshaw wonders what kind of an advantage there is in being alive and knowing that one too faces inevitable death. If there were some hint of life after death, the living might indeed have some kind of hope.

Unfortunately, such is not the case. Nor is Qoheleth sure that human death is any more exalted than that of the beasts. Human and beast share a single fate; both return to the dust from which they were made. Again he advises enjoyment of life as it unfolds. This is the only assurance of happiness that one can have and it is an assurance within the reach of all.

Crenshaw concludes his study of Qoheleth by tracing again Qoheleth's movement of thought. He went from "enthusiastic endorsement of life to flirtation with death as rest, from sheer pleasure over life's sweetness to hatred of life under certain circumstances. Truly, Qoheleth did not succumb to despair without a flight."[67] The despair of which Crenshaw speaks did not lead Qoheleth to the brink of suicide. It never seems to have entered his mind. He shuns this total rejection of life in favor of a modest but powerful solution: take the little that life may offer and live it to the hilt.

6
Sirach And Wisdom

The Book of Sirach, like the Book of Proverbs before it, is a collection of wisdom material intended for instruction. It contains a short preface written by the grandson and translator of a sage known as Ben Sira. The author appears to have been a man steeped in the prophetic as well as the sapiential traditions of ancient Israel. His grandson preserved these teachings by translating them from the original Hebrew into Greek, Thus making the work available to a larger audience.

The book has a second title, Ecclesiasticus, which appears in some Greek and Latin manuscripts and means "of the Church." This designation is thought to have arisen from frequent use of the book within the early Church. It is not included within the collection of books which comprise the Hebrew Bible, and a large segment of the Christian community as well has considered it to be lacking the kind of authority enjoyed by Proverbs, Job, and Qoheleth. Though still respected as religious literature, Sirach is regarded to be apocryphal rather than inspired and canonical writing. The Roman Catholic community, on the other hand, acknowledging the long controversy over the question of the inclusion of this book in the canon, regards it as inspired and authoritative but classifies it as deuterocanonical.

The Wisdom of Solomon, also referred to simply as Wisdom, is another of those books about which there has been controversy. Not everyone considers it canonical, and it is, therefore, listed as deutero-

canonical or as apocryphal. The book itself makes a claim for
Solomonic authorship but the very fact that it relies heavily on the
Septuagint version of earlier material illustrates that it must have
originated after that third century work. This claim of Solomonic
authorship is not intended to deceive the reader. On the contrary,
ancient authors who wrote within certain traditions often assumed
the name of the authority associated with that tradition.

The real author probably wrote from Alexandria in Egypt to
other Jews of the diaspora who may have been wavering in their faith
because of the strong Greek influences in their lives. This new
intellectual atmosphere seems to have threatened older expressions
of Israel's non-philosophical religion. The author sets out to show
the wisdom and depth of Israel's faith and thereby to strengthen his
co-religionists in their commitments.

Wisdom and Torah in Sirach

Von Rad devotes an entire chapter to "The Wisdom of Jesus
Sirach."[68] He begins by noting the author's opening statement regarding wisdom (1:1–10). This acknowledgement of the inscrutabil-
ity of divine wisdom is followed by reflection about the primeval
nature of wisdom. Only in v 10 is there mention of wisdom as a
human characteristic. This latter type is quite different from either
divine or primeval wisdom, for it is intimately linked with human
conduct. Even when the focus is on human behavior, the image of
wisdom is very ambiguous. At times it seems to be the fruit of human
striving and accomplishment. At other times it is more like some
mysterious ordering power within the universe which calls out to
women and men and leads them to knowledge of the world and of
life itself. This image is not unlike the one of Lady Wisdom found
within Proverbs 7—9.

The first important theme addressed is fear of God. According
to von Rad, Sirach interprets this fear, the great goal of human life,
quite apart from earlier wisdom thought. In "old wisdom" such fear
was an admission of human dependence upon God and of the basic
human responsibility to conform to the divine will. Sirach describes
this description in an entirely different manner. It is not so much an
attitude toward God as it is an experiential reality. This newer

understanding does not deny the former. Rather, it expands it, and in this expansion Sirach relates the fear of God with Torah.

Von Rad is very clear in his rejection of any interpretation of Sirach that claims that this sage departs from old teaching by replacing experiential wisdom with the Torah. He insists that the didactic material in Sirach arises from a careful direct observation and evaluation of human experience and not from the written law. He does not deny that Torah plays a very significant role in Sirach's thought, but it is a secondary role. Like the wisdom teachers before him, Sirach recognized the relationship between fear of God and the divine will. The difference is that here he speaks to an age wherein the divine will is almost identical with the written law.

Von Rad continues, "It is not that wisdom is overshadowed by the superior power of the Torah, but, vice versa, that we see Sirach endeavouring to legitimize and to interpret Torah from the realm of understanding characteristic of wisdom."[69] The question is not "How can wisdom be Torah?" but rather "How can Torah be wisdom?" Sirach answers this by identifying Torah as that primeval ordering wisdom inherent in the universe from the beginning but revealed at some point in history in this new guise. Even here, Torah is secondary to primeval wisdom.

Contingency and Order in Sirach

It appears that Sirach is primarily concerned with two overarching themes: the element of contingency and the question of the existence of a hidden underlying and ruling order. Although these are distinct questions they are, nonetheless, interrelated. Utilizing the didactic technique of presenting opposite evaluations of one and the same thing, Sirach illustrates the ambiguity of appearances. What seems appropriate in one situation is totally inappropriate in another. Each situation must be analyzed individually and judged singly. The contingent character of life and of human experience prevents one from drawing up beforehand a plan of action that will guarantee success. The teaching method of Sirach, that of offering more than one course of action, does not suggest which manner of behavior is the right one but insists that there is a right way.

Both Qoheleth and Sirach agree that there is a right "time" to which contingency is subject and that divine control of that "time" is hidden from human view. They part company, however, on the question of the possibility of ever knowing this special "time." Qoheleth despairs of ever discovering it or being the recipient of its revelation. Sirach believes that whatever is not within human reach will be supplied by God.

The consideration of divine power active in ordering life leads von Rad to the question of theodicy. Sirach states, "The deeds of God are all good, they suffice in their time for all that is necessary" (39:33). The key idea here is "in their time." Unlike the visitors of Job who demanded that the power of God be understood within a definite fixed pattern, Sirach acknowledges that divine rule follows a certain order, but this order is not an inflexible norm. It is based on proper timing.

Having said all of this, von Rad asks how Sirach's teaching can best be summarized. Von Rad claims that this sage is wholly within the tradition of earlier wisdom teachers. He seeks to teach wisdom and the mastery of life. He does this by reflecting on human experience. Pointing to two or more sides possessed by every situation, he teaches that the right course of action can be found only in the situation of decision. Women and men must be in constant dialogue with life. Von Rad takes this one step further when he states that Sirach is particularly concerned with the relationship between human beings and God. This is especially demonstrated in the final section of the book (44—50) where the author praises the ancestors of Israel. It was fidelity to their relationship with God that merited the honor that has been given them. Sirach presents these examples of piety for the purpose of instruction. They are the ones who have succeeded at life. They are the models to be followed.

Sirach's perception of human beings is a very positive one. They are surrounded by great mysteries and inescapable contingencies, but they are nonetheless secure in a beneficent divine order. As they strive for piety and fear of God they become what they were meant to be and the sources of wisdom and knowledge are open to them. This kind of active faith is a factor in education for life. "Whoever seeks God receives instruction" (32:14).

Von Rad does not deal directly with the theology of the Book of Wisdom. It is only in his chapter entitled "The Polemic Against

Idols"[70] that he treats it. His emphasis there is the folly of worshiping images, and it is within this context that he adverts to anything within the book.

Whybray, in *The Intellectual Tradition of the Old Testament,* limits the scope of his consideration to those books included within the category of canonical books. The ones that are termed deuterocanonical or apocryphal play no part in his study. Hence, his book has nothing to say about either Sirach or Wisdom.

Judaism Confronts Hellenism

Crenshaw's collection, *Studies in Ancient Israelite Wisdom,* does include essays which deal with the wisdom tradition in the broader sense. Alexander Di Lella's article "Conservative and Progressive Theology: Sirach and Wisdom"[71] is one such example.

Di Lella begins by describing these two books as illustrative of how Judaism in the first and second centuries before Christ responded to the crisis of Hellenization. This was a time of turmoil and confusion in both Palestine and the diaspora. The accomplishments and glories of Hellenism not only enriched the Jews but also threatened to undermine their ancient beliefs. Adaptation and acculturation often resulted in accommodation and compromise. The authors of Sirach and Wisdom speak to this same crisis but from two different points of view.

The designations "conservative" and "progressive" are attributed to Sirach and Wisdom respectively. Because these two words are used in various ways, Di Lella feels that it is important that the reader understand how he is using them in the article. Thus he defines his terms. According to him, conservative is "characterized by a tendency to preserve or keep unchanged the truths and answers of the past because only these are adequate as solutions for the present problems."[72] Progressive is "characterized by a tendency to reexamine, rephrase, or adapt the truths and answers of the past in order to make them relevant to present problems."[73] From these two perspectives, i.e., conservative and progressive, Di Lella examines how the books treat (1) an attitude toward Hellenistic philosophy, (2) anthropology, (3) earthly retribution and an afterlife.

Di Lella agrees with those scholars who consider Sirach the

"prototype of the Sadducees." Like them, Sirach is conservative with respect to the law, the prophets and the other traditions of ancient Israel. What he says about anthropology and retribution is very consistent with that tradition.

Sirach appears to have been well acquainted with the effects of Hellenization. He must have known the crises that tore at the hearts of his co-religionists. Convinced of the value of Greek culture, they questioned the adequacy of Israelite religion. It was to this situation that he addressed his teaching, which was not so much an attack on Hellenism as a defense of Judaism. He tried to show that true wisdom was to be found in Israelite faith, not in Greek humanism. He utilized the time-honored technique of calling on the past to instruct the present, and the truth of Israel's past was contained within the sacred traditions of the elders. Jews did not have to apologize for their heritage in the face of Greek splendor, for they possessed in their religion a splendor that far surpassed mere human achievement. Greek speculation could never rival the revelation of the God of Israel.

The second theme highlighted by Di Lella is anthropology. Although the Book of Sirach has been transmitted in a Greek version, it is very clear that the original vocabulary and thought categories were Hebrew. Words that are often translated "flesh," "breath," "soul," "spirit," and "heart" generally have the same range of meanings as in other Hebrew writings. Sirach does not picture the human person in a dualistic manner. He does not think in terms of body and soul, flesh and spirit. Rather, he sees the human person as a vital unity that can be perceived from various perspectives.

Di Lella's final consideration is that of retribution. The predominant view at the time of Sirach has come to be called the Deuteronomic theory of retribution. Stated simply, it claims that obedience to the law will be rewarded with material prosperity and that failure to observe the law will be punished with adversity and early death. The early articulation of this theory allowed for exceptions to the rule. Suffering was explained in different ways. It appears that by the time of Sirach an almost mathematical equation had developed: virtue = prosperity; guilt = suffering. The factors of the equation could also be reversed: prosperity = virtue; suffering = guilt. It must be remembered that at this time in Israel's history there was no clear doctrine of afterlife. If justice was to be executed it had to take place here on earth. Although a doctrine of the resurrection of the body was beginning to take shape in some sectors of Jewish thought (cf. Dan 12; 2 12:38ff), Sirach does not seem to subscribe to it. He was not, however, inflexible in his understanding of the Deutero-nomic doctrine. He recognized that suffering might be a trial intend-ed to purify as well as a punishment that atoned.

In spite of his acknowledgement that appearances seem to disprove the universality of the doctrine of retribution, Sirach does not take any definite steps toward suggesting an afterlife where inconsistencies can be adjusted. According to him, one lives on in one's children and in one's reputation. In this respect, it is easy to see the similarity between Sirach and the later Sadducees who rejected any thought of resurrection of the dead.

The second part of Di Lella's article discusses the same three themes as they are found in the Book of Wisdom. He refers to the author as Pseudo-Solomon because, although this author identifies himself as the king who built the temple, both literary and theologi-cal evidence within the book indicate that this work is of a much later provenance.

Like Sirach, Pseudo-Solomon speaks to a Jewish community that has to deal with the onslaughts of Hellenization. While the former probably wrote in Jerusalem, the latter was most likely an Alexandrian Jew. The difference in locale as well as the fact that Wisdom was written somewhat later may account for some of the dissimilarity of approach. Though Pseudo-Solomon utilized Greek language and literary techniques in his work, he insisted that the Greek authors did not surpass the Hebrew tradition and that Juda-ism need not apologize for its beliefs and religious practices. Not only was it not inferior, but it could be rearticulated in a different language for a different age, while retaining its Jewish message. He believed further that the search for religious truth and the search for secular knowledge need not conflict. "Truth is one because God is one."[74]

The inconsistencies in Pseudo-Solomon's anthropological per-spective are noted and explained in the article. Although he em-ployed the terms and thought patterns of Greek philosophical speculation, he was still influenced by the earlier anthropological categories of his own religious tradition. This often resulted in a certain ambiguity about the range of meaning of the terms used. While the Greek words for "soul," "spirit," "mind," "body," "flesh," and "heart" appear in his teaching, they seldom bear an exclusively Greek meaning. It is clear that the task facing the author was more than merely one of translating. He was trying to harmonize two very different anthropological perspectives, hence outrightly rejecting neither one yet also representing neither one accurately. In Pseudo-Solomon one can see a man moving toward a body-soul dualism characteristic of Greek anthropology but not yet having arrived.

The third theme which Di Lella considered is retribution. Biblical Israel's struggle with this concept is evident in the diverse, even contradictory positions represented in various books. Job could neither fully accept it nor could he reject it. Although Qoheleth dismissed it as an inadequate explanation of reality, Sirach appears to have supported the theory. Only Pseudo-Solomon provides a somewhat satisfying solution to the dilemma in his doctrine of an afterlife. The good *will* be rewarded; the evil *will* be punished, if not here, then in an afterlife.

When he speaks of immortality he is proceeding from the Jewish, rather than the Greek, point of view. There is no concentration here on an immortal constitutive element in the human makeup. Rather, belief in the justice of God has forced the issue. The righteousness of God is enduring, and the just who are faithful to their covenant with this righteous God will enjoy the rewards of their faithfulness. Therefore, life after death is the answer to the question of retribution.

Di Lella summarized his interpretation of Pseudo-Solomon in four points:

1. The author's view of a body-soul composite is relevant to his teaching on immortality.

2. Immortality is a gift bestowed on the person as a unity.

3. It is not clear how immortality will be bestowed.

4. Because the focus is on the whole person, it seems likely that final retribution will include resurrection of the body.

The Preservation of Tradition

The last article to be reviewed is Edmond Jacob's "Wisdom and Religion in Sirach." It appears in *Israelite Wisdom* and offers what might best be called a nuanced point of view. While many scholars identify Sirach as the grandfather of the final editor, Jacob claims that it is not certain whether he is father, grandfather or perhaps an even more distant relative. In addition to this, the name of the final editor is not clear. The Hebrew of Sirach 50:27 is uncertain, and the name could be either Jesus, as most believe, or Simon, as Jacob also proposes. In describing the religious milieu of the time he highlights some of the tensions facing the people. "Judaism has undergone a transformation, but was this transformation not going to change into alienation; and that which one considered as progress from many points of view, was it not going to become an infidelity? Was wisdom going to become an ally of religion, or develop outside and against it?"[75] It was to such questions that Sirach directed his teaching.

The issue of whether or not Israel had established schools which were conducted by sages is discussed briefly. Jacob acknowledges the opposition to this view especially as found in Whybray's work, but he concludes that Sirach probably was a school master and he refers to 51:23 in support of this view. "Draw near to me, you who are untaught, and lodge in my school." He agrees with those who believe that there were some schools intent on facilitating the absorption of Hellenistic culture and others committed to the preservation of ancestral Jewish heritage. He would classify Sirach with the latter. This picture of Sirach as a preserver of tradition resembles Di Lella's designation of him as conservative.

His overview of the political history of the period is enlightening *NB* and suggests possible motivation behind Sirach's teaching. The Seleucids had overthrown the Ptolomies and had administered rather lenient control over the Jewish people who had lent support in the overthrow. The Jewish historian Josephus has left a record of some of the favors that the Jews enjoyed. In spite of this fact internal tensions developed between competing priestly families and between

Jews and Samaritans. These were intensified when the Greek over-
lords felt compelled to increase taxes and exert more external control. Thus, some rights were denied and religious freedom was
threatened. These circumstances most likely influenced the force
with which Sirach advanced his views.

Jacob insists that the most significant theme of the work is
wisdom. He agrees that fear of God occupies an important place, but
he disagrees with von Rad and others who claim that it is central to
the book. Fear of God may well be considered the beginning of
wisdom, but it is not, according to Sirach, the point of departure in
one's search. Rather, wisdom leads one to see fear of God as one
manifestation of wisdom itself. Even the literary structure of the
book illustrates the prominence of the wisdom theme. The book can
be divided into three major sections, each delineated by a sapiential
hymn. The hymns are found in 1:1–10, 24:1–31, and 51:13–30.

A careful analysis of these pericopes has enabled Jacob to arrive
at three major conclusions about Sirach's theology of wisdom. First,
wisdom is initially manifested in creation. It is because of wisdom
that creation is one, although this is a unity in duality. Sirach
perceives reality as a harmony of opposites: good vis-à-vis evil, life
vis-à-vis death, light vis-à-vis gloom, etc. The balance of opposites
results in an order or harmony that Sirach calls "glory." Creation
reveals this glory which is also associated with the glory of God
proclaimed again and again within the liturgical tradition of Israel.
This interpretation of Sirach's attention to opposites differs in its
nuancing from von Rad's effort to explain it as Sirach's dealing with
contingency.

The second conclusion which Jacob perceives in his study of
this theology of wisdom is the importance of history. It is common-
place to recognize the ahistorical nature of sapiential literature.
Sirach, on the contrary, has utilized the early history of Israel to
show how fidelity to Torah led the ancestors into a deeper perception
of life and, thereby into a more profound wisdom. As a theologian of
wisdom and not primarily of Torah, Sirach places the covenant
within the broader reality of creation rather than linking creation
with covenant. Jacob agrees with von Rad here.

Jacob's third and final conclusion deals with the fear of God as
a manifestation of wisdom. Building on the work of earlier scholars,

Jacob agrees that trust and humility are principal aspects of fear of God. Judging these to be attitudes which are more prophetic than sapiential attitudes, he links them with Sirach's posture toward prayer. Fear of God is a disposition that manifests itself in inner piety as well as in public praise. The temple liturgy is the point of convergence of fear and praise, and it is the vehicle for the expression of "glory."

Jacob sees Sirach as a sage who never allowed wisdom to usurp the place of God who is hidden and far surpasses any wisdom that humans might attain. He stands in awe of the Torah but never in such a way as to give it a prominence it does not deserve. He perceives a harmony and balance in life and does not wish to create any conflict. He has no intention of inaugurating one school of thought in opposition to any other. Rather, Sirach has made every effort to safeguard the unity between the diverse factors within Judaism and between Judaism and the Greek world. Here Jacob would disagree with scholars such as Di Lella who see Sirach as a pre-Sadducee. Sirach sought a common ground in a world in which the ground seemed to be shifting.

7
Wisdom Influences?

The publication in 1953 of von Rad's study, "The Joseph Narrative and Ancient Wisdom," opened the door for a search for wisdom influence and teaching in sections of the Hebrew tradition seldom before associated with wisdom.[76] The result of this trend was a flood of articles claiming that sapiential themes and vocabulary play a significant role in historical as well as prophetic material. These findings were not always welcomed wholeheartedly. Many scholars believed that some of the claims were ill-founded and that the arguments that supported them were questionable. The following chapter is not intended to be a thorough examination of the question. It simply presents representative examples of the work that has been done and continues to be done in this area of research in order to show its development and direction. Only the thesis and major arguments of each article reviewed here will be stated. This focus may best illustrate the position of the individual author in respect to other scholarly opinions.

Opposing Views

Studies in Ancient Israelite Wisdom includes articles expressive of views on both sides of the issue. They are treated here in the chronological order in which they appeared in the scholarly world. The first article in the final section of this collection of essays is Johannes Fichtner's "Isaiah Among the Wise." In it the author articulates the view which prevailed as late as 1949. "In the spiritual history of Israel, there are few so completely antithetical phenomena as prophecy and *hokmah* (wisdom)"[77] In spite of this position, Fichtner does admit that there are many both literary and theological similarities between even the early prophets and the molders of the wisdom thinking. Both traditions advance strong ethical admonitions and consequently employ similar vocabulary and imagery. Fichtner unequivocally rejects the possibility of literary dependence. He attributes any similarity to a common stock of language and ideas in use in the ancient Near East.

His study of Amos, Hosea and Micah led him to conclude that they show no sign of hokmatic influence. These men of the countryside probably had no contact with the sophisticated sages of the court. Whatever may resemble wisdom influence he considers a later addition. The same is true of most of the other prophets. It is only when he turns to Isaiah that Fichtner discovers a relationship between the prophetic and the hokmatic traditions.

Although Isaiah clearly condemns human wisdom for its claims of excellence and independence of divine wisdom (cf.5:8–14, 21; 29:14), the prophet stands within the tradition of wisdom perspectives and articulates his vision of the future in wisdom imagery. Unlike earlier prophets who only sparingly employed sapiential vocabulary, Isaiah makes extensive use of words such as "wise," "know," "understanding," and "counsel." However, it is in his image of the future that his appropriation and application of sapiential themes is most evident. In the eschatological passages 9:1–6 and 11:1–9, the future leader is called "Wonder-Counsellor" (9:5) and is endowed with "the spirit of wisdom and of understanding, a spirit of counsel and of strength, a spirit of knowledge and of fear of the Lord" (11:2b).

Fichtner acknowledges this apparent contradiction to his thesis in this prophet who appears as both opponent and disciple of wisdom and he explains the difference in this way. Isaiah originally belonged to the sapiential class but separated himself after his call. It was his inaugural vision coupled with his understanding of the unique mission to which he was being called that alienated him from the claims of the proponents of wisdom.

Thus Fichtner maintains his thesis that the prophetic tradition was antagonistic toward the wisdom movement even though some prophets show remarkable knowledge of and use of sapiential forms.

Wisdom in the Pentateuch

As noted earlier, it was von Rad's study that spearheaded the advancement of a different point of view. Comparing the Joseph narrative with other patriarchal stories, von Rad discovered several significant differences that led him to draw the conclusions which he did. First, the very length of the narrative suggested that this is not a cycle of self-contained sagas as are the stories about Abraham, Isaac and Jacob. This is a literary unit with cohesion and internal consistency. Further, the Joseph story is not fixed to any ancestral locale such as Bethel or Shechem or to the theological themes such as promise of progeny or of land. Rather, the narrative has affinities with the Succession Narrative (2 Samuel 6 to 1 Kings 2) and other writings that can be best associated with the monarchy which exhibited a fondness for things foreign.

In the major portion of the article, von Rad highlights those characteristics within the material that he believes are akin to the wisdom tradition. He claims that the picture of Joseph that emerges is one of "a young man at his best, well-bred and finely educated, steadfast in faith and versed in the ways of the world."[78] That is the same picture that the wisdom literature holds up as a model for all to emulate. Joseph had access to the court as did the sage. However, such literary resemblance is not enough to conclude that the story belongs to the wisdom tradition. Evidence of theological affinity must be brought forward before that classification can be proposed.

Von Rad states that unlike most of the Hebrew tradition, neither the wisdom writings nor the Joseph narrative contains many specifically theological statements. The major focus in both is human accomplishment. This is not to deny the divine economy, but to view it as hidden rather than explicit. This hidden nature of the divine economy is the subject of much sapiential speculation. The ancients believed that the events of human history were subject to a law beyond the grasp of human comprehension. Von Rad claims that this belief is behind Joseph's remark to his brothers concerning God's design: "It was really for the sake of saving lives that God sent me here ahead of you" (Gen 45:5b).

Von Rad states his conclusions quite simply: "The Joseph narrative is a didactic wisdom-story which leans heavily upon influences emanating from Egypt, not only with regard to its conception of an educational ideal, but also in its fundamental theological ideas."[79]

Amos and Wisdom

Samuel Terrien's 1962 article "Amos and Wisdom" shows how far opinion had moved from Fichtner's 1949 position which denied any hokmatic relationship with the eighth century prophets. Terrien outlines eight points of correspondence between Amos and the wisdom tradition.

The prophet's acquaintance with wisdom language and speech habits is evident in his employment of consecutive numerals used in pairs. This formula constitutes the structure of the first two chapters of the book. "For three transgressions of Damascus, and for four . . ." (1:3). While the same form of numerical gradation frequently appears in wisdom literature (cf. Prov 30: 15–31), Amos is the only prophet to utilize this form of speech.

Another example of Amos' departure from the prophetic tradition and his agreement with the sapiential movement is found in his description of eschatological retribution. In general the Hebrew Scriptures view Sheol, the place of the dead, as outside of Yahweh's realm of activity. Examples of this are Isaiah 38:18, "For Sheol cannot thank you, death cannot praise you," and Psalm 88:11, "Is your steadfast love declared in the grave?" In contrast, Amos relates this divine communication, "Though they dig into Sheol, there shall my hand take them" (9:2). According to his prophet, Yahweh does exercise jurisdiction over the underworld.

Like the wisdom teachers, Amos appeals to common sense derived from reflection on empirical evidence. This differs from the usual insistence on revelation as the source of prophetic authority. Even when he does appeal to a divine communication, Amos uses language associated with the sapiential tradition (cf. 3:7).

Other instances of the use of wisdom vocabulary appear in his accusation of Israel's inability to know how to do what is right (3:10) as well as in his use of a verb which has caused interpreters some difficulty unless they interpret it as it has come to be understood in Job (1:11, cf. Jb 16:9; 18:4).

The final two examples of literary departure from prophetic usage are Amos' designation of the nation as "Isaac" rather than "Israel" (7:9, 16) and his reference to Beer-sheba (5:5; 8:14). These references suggest the proximity of Beer-sheba to Edom which was long recognized for its reputation for wisdom.

Terrien concludes his investigation by insisting that Amos not only was steeped in the prophetic tradition, but also was obviously influenced by the sapiential movement. He would argue that it is a mistake to think that various groups within Israel were alien to each other and always in situations of confrontation. While there certainly were significant differences between the sacral, prophetic and sapiential leaders, they all lived in the same and mutually interacting environment and drew from a common store of literary and theological understandings and expressions.

Exaggerated Claims

Finally, James Crenshaw, in "Method in Determining Wisdom Influence Upon 'Historical' Literature," an article previously discussed in Chapter 1, outlines some methodological principles that should be considered before one presumes any strictly sapiential influence in other than the recognized wisdom literature. First, Crenshaw insists upon the importance of definition. If one is not discriminating, perspectives and literary expression that may enjoy some similarity could soon be reduced to the same classification. He defines wisdom itself as "the quest for self-understanding in terms of relationships with things, people and the Creator"[80] and then distinguishes between wisdom literature, wisdom tradition and wisdom thinking.

The second principle set forth concerns the stylistic or ideological characteristics of the literature. The presence of vocabulary that is considered "wisdom" is not enough to lead one to conclude to wisdom influence. Such a tendency totally ignores the fact that a culture uses the same language in a variety of ways. Frequency of appearance cannot presume uniformity of usage.

A third principle follows closely upon the second. Whenever some vocabulary, phrase or motif is found outside of wisdom literature, it is important to decide whether the accepted sapiential meaning has been retained or modified. Next, one must remember the apparent negative attitude toward wisdom which is found in so much of the Hebrew tradition.

Finally, wisdom thinking itself underwent recognizable development. Different life situations evoked different responses. Israel changes as a nation, and religious as well as political forces influenced its policies and ideologies. Caution must be exercised as one traces lines of influence.

Crenshaw applies these five methodological observations to three works that identify certain biblical material as sapiential narrative. They are: "The Joseph Narrative and Ancient Wisdom" by von Rad, *The Succession Narrative* by Whybray, and " 'Wisdom' in the Book of Esther" by Talmon. After a short critique of each he concludes that their claims of wisdom influence are exaggerated but that some of the findings of these studies illustrate the error of a rigid compartmentalizing of Israelite society. Israel's responses to life rose out of a common cultural stock which accounts for much of the similarity in articulation.

Micah—Rural Elder

Israelite Wisdom also contains studies showing the relationship between wisdom thought and prophetic writing. Hans Walter Wolff declares his indebtedness to the essay "Amos and Wisdom" by Terrien. It was influential in his own work on Amos as well as on his article "Micah the Moreshite—The Prophet and His Background." Limiting his focus to three passages of undisputed authenticity, Wolff sets out to show that the prophet was one of the elders of rural Moresheth. It was in this capacity that he ventured to Jerusalem where he entered into conflict with the leaders of that great city. If Micah was indeed an elder, many characteristics of language and appearance would be explained. Wolff points out six such characteristics.

Micah addressed the "heads of the house of Jacob and the rulers of the house of Israel" (3:1, 9). He speaks to neither king nor royal official but to the members of the leading circles of Jerusalem who probably exercised judicial authority in competition with his own. This theory is strengthened when one recalls that Micah described his commission as one of justice (3:8). The execution of justice was the prerogative and responsibility of the judicial authority.

The third point in Wolff's argument is the fact that Micah sees himself as the representative of his compatriots. He speaks of "my people" (1:9; 2:9; 3:3, 5). Jerusalem is called "the gate of my people." It was at the city gate that judgment was passed. It was through Jerusalem and the decisions passed within it that the people of Moresheth received justice. Micah, an elder of the land, went to Jerusalem as an advocate of that justice.

Wolff highlights three different examples of Micah's use of a literary style associated with the countryside. He uses imagery akin to peasant life (3:2–3) and he adopts the form of the mourning ceremony which originated within rural communities (1:8). Finally, he employs a literary style very much like that of Amos (2:6–11; cf. Am 3:3–8).

The conclusion drawn by Wolff is that the intellectual background of the prophet Micah is to be found in the sphere of life of the elders of Judah. Wolff does not say that Micah was a sage nor that he was strongly influenced by the wisdom movement. Rather, he speaks of the milieu of the prophet, the intellectual environment. It seems that scholars have moved from the two poles of either denying any relationship between wisdom and other parts of Scripture, e.g., Fichtner, or of classifying certain narratives as sapiential works, e.g., von Rad, to a third position. This finely nuanced position acknowledges a rich and complex society with several traditions drawing from a common treasury of ideas and expressions and influencing each other while at the same time remaining significantly distinct.

The Wisdom of Jeremiah

Two other studies in this collection of essays espouse this same view. The first is "The Epistemological Crisis of Israel's Two Histories (Jer 9:22–23)" by Walter Brueggemann. He begins by stating that recent wisdom studies have shown that the sapiential tradition is not on the periphery but rather at the heart of the reflective life of Israel. He characterizes wisdom as "the deposit of the best observations coming from a long history of reflection on experience."[81] When a society faces the prospect of collapse, epistemological conventions must give way to new ones. Jeremiah's insistence upon new perspectives was met with obduracy from the Jerusalem establishment. This was the conflict that tore at the heart of the prophet and of the nation. It was not so much a struggle against wisdom as it was a question of which wisdom was to prevail. Was it that of the establishment which relied on wisdom, might and riches, or was it the wisdom of Yahweh which insisted upon steadfast love, justice and righteousness?

Brueggemann shows that the prophet used sapiential language and forms as he refuted the false security of the monarchy. Jeremiah's message is clear. Self-contained wisdom makes false promises. It pretends to grant life and in reality brings death. Only "foolish" fidelity to Yahweh is true wisdom and it alone can guarantee life.

A Response to Skepticism

In the second article, "The Servant's Knowledge in Isaiah 40—55," James Ward sketches the dramatic change in scholarly perception of the importance of wisdom. Formerly critics gave priority to the prophets whenever they compared their writings with those of the historians, the lawgivers, the psalmists and the sages. Today the position is quite the reverse. Scholars agree that the Yahwistic and the Elohistic traditions of the Pentateuch preceded the canonical prophets who were then greatly influenced by these earlier traditions. Likewise, the main types of psalms predated the prophets. Finally, there is a growing consensus that the prophets were influenced by the wisdom tradition.

Ward's research attempts to show that Isaiah 40—55 is a response to the intellectual skepticism present in Israel and expressed in books like Job and Qoheleth. This skepticism did not question the existence of God but, rather, God's effective involvement in human lives. Isaiah's response to this attitude was a defense of divine wisdom.

Ward sets out to show Isaiah's belief that only Israel, among all the nations of the world, possessed a prophetic interpretation of history. The greatness of Yahweh revealed in Israel's history could be recognized only in the light of prophetic insight and interpretation. These tasks were ascribed to the servant of Yahweh, a figure that symbolized the entire people. It was the knowledge of this servant that would make many righteous. The servant would provide the necessary interpretation for others that they might see the divine activity in the lives of the people.

Like Brueggemann, Ward presumes a basic intellectual milieu within which prophet and sage alike were immersed. Mutual influence is less a case of literary borrowing than it is a sharing of common cultural roots and of sensitivity to the contemporary scene. There is no denial here of clear differentiation among various groups within society. Ward merely acknowledges a complex but common intellectual milieu in biblical Israel which acted upon the minds and hearts of the people, and from this common milieu emerged various insights and religious perspectives.

A Didactic Book

The last article to be considered is another example of how a piece of biblical literature defies narrow classification. In "Jonah: a Mašal?" George Landes advances the view that the book was written in a form that is usually associated with the wisdom school. Scholars have frequently labeled Jonah a parable, but they have not gone further and said that this parable is a form of a *mašal.* Landes attempts to do just that.

He begins by describing and defining *mašal.* Although the word has generally been translated as "proverb," Landes states that precise defining is a difficult task because *mašal* appears to have no fixed literary form. The closest he comes to a definition is to say that it is "related to the ideas of likeness, resemblance, and comparison."[82] After analyzing five examples of the form (popular proverb, satirical taunt poem, prophetic-type oracular poem descriptive of weal or woe, didactic poem, and allegorizing parabolic fable), he examines the Book of Jonah in light of his findings.

As a work of literary art, Jonah is unique among the books of the Hebrew Scriptures. It does not fit into any of the categories provided by form criticism. Landes scrutinizes the content and function of the book in order to determine whether or not it corresponds to his description of *mašal* and can, therefore, be so considered.

It becomes clear from the outset that the intention of the author is didactic. Three of Landes' conclusions support this: a twofold structural arrangement of the content and themes; the symbolic function of certain features in the content; the employment of questions as a rhetorical device.

The author has fashioned the book by means of parallel structures. There is an overall parallelism between Jonah in the first two chapters and Jonah in the last two. The same is true with regard to the sailors in the beginning of the book and the Ninevites at the end. The second parallelism is evident in the relation of God to Jonah and the sailors and then God to Jonah and the Ninevites. This parallelism highlights the difference between Jonah and the other actors in the drama.

The Ninevites were hated enemies of ancient Israel. It is ironic that the author of the book has presented them in the manner in which he has. This nation had come to represent all that Israel abhorred. They were a people who scorned the worship of Yahweh and threatened the very survival of Yahweh's special nation. The author could not have chosen a better symbol for disbelief and sinfulness. On the other hand, Jonah represented a fierce nationalism that was both religious and political. One could not miss the intention of the author in fashioning the characters in this way.

Finally, the artful use of questions leads the reader to the conclusions intended by the author. Jonah has refused to be a minister of God's deliverance and has rejected that same mercy in his own life. In contrast to him, the Ninevites responded with contrition and repentance and God was prodigal with mercy and forgiveness. The book has accomplished a twofold didactic purpose. It has offered penetrating food for thought and has put forward a model to be followed.

Having provided evidence for calling the book a *mašal*, Landes next asks the question of provenance. From which particular circle did the book originate? He proceeds to show that the majority of *mašal*-texts stem from two sources: the prophetic and the sapiential. Agreeing with Crenshaw that certain criteria must be strictly followed before one rushes to the conclusion that a book should be classified as sapiential literature, Landes weighs the evidence he has uncovered and concludes that Jonah was a prophetic *mašal*, influenced by prophetic concerns.

Once again contemporary scholarship has shown that the literature of biblical Israel cannot always be neatly classified, and our understanding of the context out of which the literature arose must be free of too restrictive categories. At the same time, differentiations must be acknowledged and nuanced. Biblical research has shown itself committed not only to discovery but to refinement as well.

Postscript

Although this volume is entitled *What Are They Saying About Wisdom Literature?* and the intent of the author was to give some idea of what they are saying, in no way have these short chapters captured the extent of the scholarship being done. New insights and deeper probings into older ones are constantly being pursued. The field has expanded significantly and continues to do so. The reader is encouraged to consult the works treated here as well as the studies referred to by the various authors in order to be further enriched and to appreciate that elusive reality known as wisdom.

Notes

1. Gerhard von Rad, *Old Testament Theology*, Vol. I (New York: Harper & Row, 1967), 418.
2. ————, *Wisdom in Israel* (Nashville: Abingdon, 1972), 71.
3. *Ibid.*, 128f.
4. *Ibid.*, 148.
5. R.N. Whybray, *The Intellectual Tradition in the Old Testament* (Berlin: Walter de Gruyter, 1974), 72f.
6. *Ibid.*, 70.
7. Von Rad, *op cit.*, 291.
8. Whybray, *op. cit.*, 6.
9. *Ibid.*, 7.
10. James L. Crenshaw, *Studies in Ancient Israelite Wisdom* (New York: KTAV, 1976), ix.
11. *Ibid.*, ix.
12. *Ibid.*, 484.
13. *Ibid.*, 26.
14. *Ibid.*, 34.
15. John G. Gammie, Walter A. Brueggemann, W. Lee Humphreys, James M. Ward, eds., *Israelite Wisdom: Theological and Literary Essays in Honor of Samuel Terrien* (Missoula, Montana: Scholars Press, 1978), 35.
16. Roland E. Murphy, "Wisdom Theses," *Wisdom and Knowledge: Papin Festschrift*, J. Armenti, ed. (Philadelphia: Villanova Press, 1976), 187–200.
17. Von Rad, *op. cit.*, 106f.
18. Murphy, *op. cit.*, 197.
19. Von Rad, *op. cit.*, 97ff.
20. *Ibid.*, 139.
21. *Ibid.*, 126.

22. *Ibid.,* 106.

23. Ibid.

24. Von Rad, *op. cit.,* 34.

25. Cf. von Rad, *Old Testament Theology,* Vol. I, 48–56.

26. Gerhard von Rad, *The Problem of the Hexateuch and Other Essays* (New York: McGraw-Hill Book Company, 1966), 71.

27. Crenshaw, *op. cit.,* 440.

28. Cf. Walter Brueggemann, *In Man We Trust* (Richmond: John Knox Press, 1972).

29. Crenshaw, op. cit., 16–20.

30. ———, *"Wisdom in Israel* by Gerhard von Rad," *Religious Studies Review* 2, n.2)

31. ———, *Gerhard von Rad* (Waco: Word, 1978).

32. ———, *Studies,* 20.

33. Pages 102–111.

34. The following is a summary of Scott's thought found on page 34 of *Studies.*

35. *Ibid.,* 99.

36. *Ibid.,* 16.

37. Gammie, etc., *op.cit.,* 37.

38. Berend Gemser, "Motive Clauses in Old Testament Law," *Vetus Testamentum Supplement,* I (1953), 50–66.

39. J.P. Audet, "Origines comparées de la double tradition de la loi et de la sagesse dans la proche-orient ancient," *Acten Internationalen Orientalisten-Kongresses,* 1 (Moscow, 1962), 352–357.

40. E. Gerstenberger, *Wesen und Herkunft des 'apodiktischen Rechts, 'Wissenschaftliche Monographie zum Alten und Neuen Testament,* 20 (Neukirchen-Vluyn: Neukirchener, 1965).

41. Wolfgang Richter, *Recht und Ethos. Studien zum Alten und Neuen Testament,* 15 (Munchen: Kösel, 1966).

42. Von Rad, *Wisdom in Israel,* Chapter III.

43. *Ibid.,* 27.

44. *Ibid.,* 74.

45. Whybray, *Intellectual Tradition,* 57.

46. ———, *Wisdom in Proverbs. Studies in Biblical Theology,* 45 (London: SCM, 1965).

47. Crenshaw, *Studies,* 329.

48. Patrick Skehan, "The Seven Columns of Wisdom's House in Proverbs 1–9," *CBQ* 9 (1947), 190–198.

49. Crenshaw, *op. cit.,* 330.

50. *Ibid.,* 175, n. 1.

51. *Ibid.*, 178.
52. *Ibid.*, 179.
53. *Ibid.*, 183.
54. *Ibid.*, 208.
55. *Ibid.*, 209.
56. *Ibid.*, 210.
57. *Ibid.*
58. Gammie, etc., *op.cit.*, 177.
59. Von Rad, *Wisdom in Israel*, 207.
60. *Ibid.*, 221.
61. *Ibid.*, 225.
62. Crenshaw, *Studies*, 350.
63. *Ibid.*, 366.
64. Whybray, *Intellectual Tradition*, 67.
65. Crenshaw, *Studies*, 385.
65a. *Ibid.*
66. *Ibid.*, 265.
67. Gammie, etc., *op. cit.*, 211.
68. Von Rad, *Wisdom in Israel*, Chapter XIII.
69. *Ibid.*, 245.
70. *Ibid.*, 177–185.
71. Crenshaw, *Studies*, 401.
72. *Ibid.*, 401.
73. *Ibid.*
74. *Ibid.*, 410.
75. Gammie, etc., *op. cit.*, 248.
76. Herman Gunkel had already firmly established the category of "wisdom psalm." Cf. Herman Gunkel, *Einleitung in die Psalmen* (Göttingen: Vandenhoeck and Ruprecht, 1933).
77. Crenshaw, *Studies*, 429.
78. *Ibid.*, 442.
79. *Ibid.*, 447.
80. *Ibid.*, 484.
81. Gammie, etc., *op. cit.*, 86.
82. *Ibid.*, 139.

Further Reading

Chapter 1: Definition

Crenshaw, James L. *Old Testament Wisdom: An Introduction*. Atlanta: John Knox Press, 1981. An introduction to the wisdom literature of biblical Israel intended as an introductory textbook. Treatment of individual books is preceded by general essays.

McKane, William. *Prophets and Wise Men*. Naperville: A.R. Allenson, 1965. An exploration and examination of the causes behind the tensions and incompatibility between the prophets and the sages. The author explains the apparent complexity of the book as stemming from the detailed nature of the arguments.

Morgan, Donn F. *Wisdom in the Old Testament Traditions*. Atlanta: John Knox Press, 1981. An overall view of wisdom and Israelite religion with the purpose of discovering wisdom elements in other than the wisdom literature. The author holds that only such a comprehensive study will reveal the nature and scope of the wisdom tradition.

Murphy, Roland. *The Forms of the Old Testament Literature*. Grand Rapids: Eerdmans, 1981. The first in a series of twenty-four works. It is a form-critical analysis of the books of the wisdom literature, fundamentally exegetical with a succinct history of the scholarship pertinent to the issues of the respective books.

Scott, R.B.Y. *The Way of Wisdom*. New York: Macmillan, 1971. A lucid non-technical account of the content, historical background and current relevance of the wisdom tradition. An extensive treatment of wisdom vocabulary is a major part of the work.

Skehan, Patrick W. *Studies in Israelite Poetry and Wisdom.* Washington, D.C.: Catholic Biblical Association of America, 1971. A collection of scholarly essays addressing several issues associated with the wisdom tradition as well as textual and structural questions related to the literature.

Chapter 2: Setting

Bryce, Glendon. *A Legacy of Wisdom.* Cranbury, N.J.: Associated University Press, 1979. A comprehensive study of the relationship and contribution of Egyptian wisdom traditions to those of biblical Israel. The history of tradition transmission and development is treated at great length.

Brueggemann, Walter. *In Man We Trust.* Atlanta: John Knox Press, 1972. The author develops the idea that the monarchy was the locus of the growth and maturation of the wisdom movement. He further treats neglected themes such as culture, human accomplishments and the affirmation of life.

Chapter 3: Proverbs

McKane, William. *Proverbs.* Philadelphia: Westminster, 1970. A thorough analysis of the Book of Proverbs with a comprehensive introduction. This introduction includes a study of the ancient Near Eastern wisdom traditions and their relationship to Proverbs.

Scott, R.B.Y. *Proverbs and Ecclesiastes.* Garden City, N.Y.: Doubleday, 1965. An extensive introduction to the wisdom movement and its literature followed by a new translation of both Proverbs and Ecclesiastes and respective commentary.

Whybray, R.N. *Wisdom in Proverbs.* Naperville: A.R. Allenson, 1965. A study of the aphoristic form of proverbs used for the education of youth. The author seeks to show Israel's dependence upon an earlier tradition which was gradually modified.

Chapter 4: Job

Bergant, Dianne. *Job and Ecclesiastes.* Wilmington, Delaware: Michael Glazier, 1982. A theological commentary on both books intended to present the findings of comtemporary scholarship for the non-technical reader. Contemporary applications are made whenever possible.

Habel, Norman C. *The Book of Job*. Cambridge: University Press, 1975. A non-technical commentary that conveys the findings of modern scholarship. The author provides literary and philosophical background to the book in an introduction that also discusses dating and the literary state of the text.

Pope, Marvin. *Job*. Garden City, N.Y.: Doubleday, 1973. A volume in the Anchor Bible Series that follows that format, an extensive introduction, new translation and textual and literary notes. The author offers significant insight to the study of linguistic and literary issues.

Westermann, Claus. *The Structure of the Book of Job*. Philadelphia: Westminster, 1977. A form-critical analysis of the lament form which appears to be the prominent genre of the Book of Job. The author claims that the form provides the key for understanding the book.

Chapter 5: Qoheleth

Bergant, Dianne, *Job and Ecclesiastes*. Wilmington, Delaware: Michael Glazier, 1982. A theological commentary on both books intended to present the findings of contemporary scholarship for the non-technical reader. Contemporary applications are made whenever possible.

Gordis, Robert. *Koheleth, the Man and His World*. New York: Jewish Theological Seminary, 1955. A series of essays on the literary as well as theological issues of the book along with a translation and commentary of the text of Qoheleth.

Scott, R.B.Y. *Proverbs and Ecclesiastes*. Garden City, N.Y.: Doubleday, 1965. An extensive introduction to the wisdom movement and its literature followed by a new translation of both Proverbs and Ecclesiastes and respective commentary.

Chapter 6: Sirach and Wisdom

Clarke, Ernest G. *The Wisdom of Solomon*. Cambridge: University Press, 1973. A volume in the Cambridge Series which provides brief sections on dating, authorship and purpose of the book. The major section of the book is devoted to commentary.

Reese, James M. *Hellenistic Influence on the Book of Wisdom and Its Consequences.* Rome: Biblical Institute, 1970. A scholarly analysis consisting of a comparison of the vocabulary and style of the book with that of the Septuagint. This is followed by an examination of the literary genre.

Snaith, John G. *Ecclesiasticus.* Cambridge: University Press, 1974. A commentary in which the findings of modern scholarship are made available to the general reader.

Chapter 7: Wisdom Influences?

Perdue, Leo G. *Wisdom and Cult.* Missoula, Montana: Scholars Press, 1977. A systematic examination of the relationship between the cult and wisdom. Comprehensive treatment is given to the view of cult as found in Egyptian wisdom as well as that of Mesopotamia.

Weinfeld, Moshe. *Deuteronomy and the Deuteronomic School.* Oxford: Clarendon Press, 1972. The author attempts to show that Deuteronomy originated in a circle of scribes and sages in the period of Hezekiah-Josiah. Attention is given to the homiletic framework of the book as well as the liberal vein of the Deuteronomic code.

Whedbee, J. *Isaiah and Wisdom.* Nashville: Abingdon, 1971. An analysis of the speeches of the prophet which represent different types of prophetic discourse. The author concludes that Isaiah was significantly influenced by the wisdom traditions.

Wolff, Hans Walter. *Amos the Prophet.* Philadelphia: Fortress, 1973. A form-critical analysis of the language and style of the prophet. The author asserts that the prophet drew heavily on wisdom literature. The book is clear and non-technical.